E R I E S

MICROSOFT®
QUICKBASIC

□ □ □ □ □

K R I S   J A M S A

PUBLISHED BY
Microsoft Press
A Division of Microsoft Corporation
16011 NE 36th Way, Box 97017, Redmond, Washington 98073-9717

Library of Congress Cataloging in Publication Data

Jamsa, Kris A.
Microsoft QuickBASIC : programmer's quick reference / Kris Jamsa.
        p.   cm.
1. BASIC (Computer program language)   2. Microsoft QuickBASIC
(Computer program)   I. Title.
QA76.73.B3J37   1989   89-3199
005.26--dc19   .   CIP
ISBN 1-55615-204-3

Printed and bound in the United States of America.

1 2 3 4 5 6 7 8 9 WAKWAK 3 2 1 0 9

Distributed to the book trade in the United States by Harper & Row.

Distributed to the book trade in Canada by General Publishing
Company, Ltd.

Distributed to the book trade outside the United States and Canada
by Penguin Books Ltd.

Penguin Books Ltd., Harmondsworth, Middlesex, England
Penguin Books Australia Ltd., Ringwood, Victoria, Australia
Penguin Books N.Z. Ltd., 182-190 Wairau Road, Auckland 10,
New Zealand

British Cataloging in Publication Data available

Project Editor: Megan Sheppard
Technical Editor: Dail Magee, Jr.

Introduction

This quick reference guide provides specifics on every Microsoft
QuickBASIC statement and function. Each entry includes a brief
description, complete syntax, details on parameters, and usually a
sample program fragment. In addition, this introduction contains information on the QuickBASIC command line options and a general
discussion of QuickBASIC types, variables, and operators.

Using the Quick Reference

Each QuickBASIC statement and function is described in the following
format:

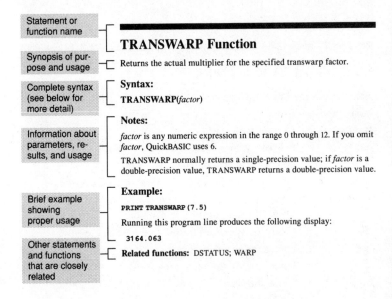

Statement or function name

Synopsis of purpose and usage

Complete syntax (see below for more detail)

Information about parameters, results, and usage

Brief example showing proper usage

Other statements and functions that are closely related

TRANSWARP Function

Returns the actual multiplier for the specified transwarp factor.

Syntax:
TRANSWARP(*factor*)

Notes:

factor is any numeric expression in the range 0 through 12. If you omit
factor, QuickBASIC uses 6.

TRANSWARP normally returns a single-precision value; if *factor* is a
double-precision value, TRANSWARP returns a double-precision value.

Example:

`PRINT TRANSWARP (7.5)`

Running this program line produces the following display:

`3164.063`

Related functions: DSTATUS; WARP

The syntax lines use the following conventions:

Convention	Description
BOLDFACE	You must enter all boldface characters as shown, unless they are enclosed in square brackets as explained below. Although QuickBASIC does not distinguish between uppercase and lowercase letters, all QuickBASIC keywords appear in uppercase letters when entered in the QuickBASIC environment.
italics	Italicized names are placeholders for information you must supply, such as a filename or a numeric value.
[*item*]	Items enclosed in square brackets are optional.
{*item1* ¦ *item2*}	Braces and a vertical bar indicate a choice among two or more items. You must choose one of the items unless the choices are enclosed in square brackets.
item...	Three dots following an item indicate that you can add more items of the same form.
item ⋮ *item*	Three dots in a column between two statements indicate that you can enter additional statements.

Command Line Options

You can use the following options when starting QuickBASIC from the DOS command line:

Option	Description
/ah	Allows dynamic arrays to exceed 64 KB
/b	Forces monochrome display
/c:*buf*	Specifies the size of the communications-port buffer
/cmd *string*	Stores *string* for later access by the COMMAND$ function (if used, must be last option specified)
file	Loads the specified BASIC source file
/g	Forces faster video output
/h	Forces maximum resolution for the video device
/l [*lib*]	Loads the specified Quick library; if *lib* is omitted, loads QB.QLB
/mbf	Causes numbers to be read and stored in Microsoft binary format
/run *file*	Runs the specified BASIC source file

QuickBASIC Types

Type	Description
INTEGER	2-byte value in the range –32,768 through 32,767
LONG	4-byte value in the range –2,147,483,648 through 2,147,483,647
SINGLE	4-byte value with 7 digits of significance
DOUBLE	8-byte value with 15 digits of significance
STRING	A sequence of up to 32,767 characters

Variable Names

A QuickBASIC variable name can contain up to 40 characters (letters, numbers, and periods). In addition, you can append one of the following characters to the name to indicate a specific variable type:

Character	Meaning
%	Integer variable
&	Long integer variable
!	Single-precision variable
#	Double-precision variable
$	String variable

Names reserved for BASIC commands, functions, or operator names cannot be used as variable names. QuickBASIC is not case sensitive. (For example, the variable names count and COUNT are identical to QuickBASIC.)

Arrays

To create a QuickBASIC array, use the following syntax:

DIM *arrayname* ([*start_index* **TO**] *last_index* [, ...]) **AS** *typename*

start_index TO *last_index* is the range of index values for the elements of the array. If you omit a starting index, QuickBASIC uses the value 0 by default. (The OPTION BASE statement allows you to set the default starting index.) The three periods indicate that QuickBASIC supports multidimensional arrays. You can specify up to 60 dimensions. For example, the following statement creates a two-dimensional array with 3 rows and 5 columns:

```
DIM box (1 TO 3, 1 TO 5) AS INTEGER
```

typename is the type of the array: INTEGER, LONG, SINGLE, DOUBLE, or STRING.

Symbolic Constants

QuickBASIC allows your programs to reference symbolic constants that you define with the CONST statement:

```
CONST size% = 255
```

QuickBASIC constant names follow the naming conventions used for variables.

Once you define a constant, you can use it throughout your program:

```
DIM a(size%) AS INTEGER
```

In so doing, you simplify future changes to your program and improve the program's readability.

Label Names

For programs that don't use line numbers, QuickBASIC allows you to use labels to reference specific locations in the program. A label name can contain up to 40 characters. Label names must begin with a letter and must end with a colon (:). Names reserved for BASIC commands, functions, or operator names cannot be used as label names. QuickBASIC is not case sensitive. (For example, the labels Handler and HANDLER are identical to QuickBASIC.)

Precedence of Operators

QuickBASIC uses the following operator-precedence table when performing operations in a given expression. Operations at the same level of precedence are performed from left to right.

Highest Precedence
(performed first)

Arithmetic:

( )	Expressions in parentheses
^	Exponentiation
−	Negation
*, /	Multiplication and division
\	Integer division
MOD	Modulus (remainder)
+, −	Addition and subtraction

Relational:

=, >, >=, <, <=, < >

Logical:

NOT
AND
OR
XOR
EQV
IMP

Lowest Precedence
(performed last)

ABS Function

Returns the absolute value of a numeric expression.

Syntax:

ABS(*numeric_expression*)

Notes:

numeric_expression is any numeric expression.

ABS always returns a positive value, regardless of whether the result of the expression is positive or negative.

ABS returns a value of the same type as *numeric_expression* (integer, long integer, double-precision, and so on).

Example:

```
PRINT "Absolute value of -3 * 5 is"; ABS(-3 * 5)
PRINT "Absolute value of 3 * 5 is"; ABS(3 * 5)
```

Running this program produces the following display:

```
Absolute value of -3 * 5 is 15
Absolute value of 3 * 5 is 15
```

ASC Function

Returns the numeric ASCII code value for the first character in a string expression.

Syntax:

ASC(*string_expression*)

Notes:

string_expression is any string expression.

Example:

```
stringvar$ = "ABC"
PRINT ASC(stringvar$)
PRINT ASC("abc")
```

Running this program produces the following display:

```
65
97
```

Related functions: CHR$

ATN Function

Returns the arctangent of the specified angle.

Syntax:

ATN(*angle*)

Notes:

angle is the angle for which you want to find the arctangent.

You can express an angle in either degrees or radians. The QuickBASIC trigonometric routines support only radians. To convert degrees to radians, use the following equation:

radians = 3.141593 * (*degrees* / 180)

Example:

```
angle = 45
PRINT "Arctangent is"; ATN(3.141593 * (angle / 180))
```

Running this program produces the following display:

```
Arctangent using radians is .6657738
```

Related functions: COS; SIN; TAN

BEEP Statement

Sounds the computer's built-in speaker.

Syntax:

BEEP

Notes:

BEEP creates a brief tone that is useful in getting the user's attention. BEEP does not affect the screen display.

Example:

```
BEEP
PRINT "Error accessing file SALES.DAT"
```

Running this program produces the following display:

(Tone from speaker)
```
Error accessing file SALES.DAT
```

BLOAD Statement

Loads a memory-image file created by the BSAVE statement into memory at the specified location.

Syntax:

BLOAD *filename*[, *offset*]

Notes:

filename is a string expression that specifies the file containing the image to load.

offset is the optional offset from the start of the data segment (or last DEF SEG), indicating where the image is to be loaded.

BLOAD and BSAVE work together to provide you with a quick and convenient way to load array values or graphics images.

Do not use BLOAD with files created by BASICA. QuickBASIC and BASICA store items differently in memory.

Example:

```
'Create an array called SALES
DIM sales (1 TO 500)

'Set the segment address to the start of SALES
DEF SEG = VARSEG(sales(1))

'Load the array using BLOAD
BLOAD "SALES.DAT", VARPTR(sales(1))

'Return to the BASIC data segment
DEF SEG
```

Related functions: VARPTR; VARSEG

Related statements: BSAVE; DEF SEG

BSAVE Statement

Copies the contents of a memory region to an output file or device.

Syntax:

BSAVE *filename*, *offset*, *length*

Notes:

filename is a string expression that specifies the file or device to which memory contents will be transferred.

offset is the location within the current segment of the first byte you want to copy.

length is the number of bytes to copy (from 0 through 65,535).

BSAVE performs a byte-by-byte copy. If you save the memory contents to a file, you can later use BLOAD to restore the memory image.

Example:

```
'Create an array with 500 elements
'Initialize the array with values from 1 through 500
DIM sales(1 TO 500)
FOR i = 1 TO 500
     sales(i) = i
NEXT i

'Set the segment address to the start of sales
DEF SEG=VARSEG(sales(1))

'Save the array using BSAVE
BSAVE "SALES.DAT", VARPTR(sales(1)), 2000

'Return to the BASIC data segment
DEF SEG
```

Related functions: VARPTR; VARSEG

Related statements: BLOAD; DEF SEG

CALL Statement (BASIC Procedures)

Transfers control to a BASIC subprogram.

Syntax:

CALL *subprogram_name* [(*argument_list*)]

or

subprogram_name [*argument_list*]

Notes:

subprogram_name is the name of a BASIC subprogram created using a SUB statement.

argument_list is a list of parameters separated by commas. The subprogram can change the values of the parameters.

You can call subprograms with or without the CALL keyword. If you omit CALL, do not place the arguments within parentheses. Also, if you omit CALL, you must use the DECLARE statement.

To prevent a subprogram from changing a parameter's value, simply place the parameter within parentheses:

```
CALL TEST (a, b, (c))
```

In this case, the subprogram can change the values of the parameters *a* and *b*, but not *c*.

Example:

```
a = 1
b = 2
CALL SwapVal(a, b)
PRINT a; b
END

SUB SwapVal(x, y)
temp = x
x = y
y = temp
END SUB
```

Running this program produces the following display:

```
 2 1
```

Related statements: CALL, CALLS; CALL ABSOLUTE; CHAIN; DECLARE

CALL, CALLS Statements
(Non-BASIC Procedures)

Transfer control to a procedure written in a programming language other than BASIC.

Syntax:

CALL *procedure* [(*parameter_list*)]

or

CALLS *procedure* [(*parameter_list*)]

or

procedure [*parameter_list*]

Notes:

procedure is the name of the procedure to call.

parameter_list is an optional list of parameters separated by commas.

QuickBASIC allows you to precede each parameter in a CALL statement with either the BYVAL or SEG keyword. BYVAL directs QuickBASIC to pass the parameter by value, which prevents the subroutine from changing the parameter. SEG directs QuickBASIC to pass the parameter as a segmented far address.

You cannot use BYVAL and SEG keywords with the CALLS statement.

Remember that routines written in C handle parameters from right to left, the opposite of the way they're handled in BASIC, Pascal, and FORTRAN.

Example:

```
DECLARE SUB Test CDECL (BYVAL value AS INTEGER)

a = 5
CALL Test(a)
END

/* separately compiled C file*/
/* compile with large memory model */
void test (int a)
{
    printf ("The value is %d\n", a);
}
```

Related statements: CALL; CALL ABSOLUTE; CHAIN; DECLARE

CALL ABSOLUTE Statement

Transfers control to a machine-language subroutine.

Syntax:

CALL ABSOLUTE ([*parameter_list*,] *offset*)

Notes:

parameter_list is an optional list of parameters separated by commas.

offset is the location within the current code segment of the start of the procedure.

To use CALL ABSOLUTE, you must use the QB.LIB library or the QB.QLB Quick library.

Example:

```
'Create a machine-language procedure and
'call it using CALL ABSOLUTE

'Array to store machine code
DIM asmroutine(1 TO 6) AS INTEGER

'Data comprising machine-code routine
DATA &H55          : ' PUSH BP
DATA &H8B,&HEC     : ' MOV BP,SP
DATA &HB4,2        : ' MOV AH,2
DATA &HB2,65       : ' MOV DL,65
DATA &HCD,&H21     : ' INT 21H
DATA &H5D          : ' POP BP
DATA &HCB,0        : ' RET

'Get array offset
offset = VARPTR(asmroutine(1))

'Change the segment to the start of the array
DEF SEG = VARSEG(asmroutine(1))

'Fill the array with machine code
FOR i = 0 TO 11
    READ asmcode
    POKE (offset + i), asmcode
NEXT i
```

(continued)

```
'Call the routine and restore the segment
CALL ABSOLUTE(VARPTR(asmroutine(1)))
DEF SEG
```

Related statements: CALL, CALLS

CALL INT86OLD Statement

Calls a DOS system service.

Syntax:

CALL INT86OLD(*interrupt_number*, *in_array*(), *out_array*())

Notes:

DOS provides a complete set of system services that your programs can access. *MS-DOS Functions* by Ray Duncan (Microsoft Press, 1988) describes these services in detail.

interrupt_number is a number (0 through 255) that corresponds to the desired DOS system service.

in_array is an 8-element integer array containing the register values in the order of AX, BX, CX, DX, BP, SI, DI, and FLAGS (*in_array*(*x*) = AX, *in_array*(*x*+1) = BX, and so on).

out_array is an 8-element array containing the register values when the DOS service completes.

To use CALL INT86OLD you must use the QB.LIB library or the QB.QLB Quick library.

Example:

```
'Create a file named TEST.DAT using interrupt 21H function 3CH
DIM inarray(1 TO 8) AS INTEGER
DIM outarray(1 TO 8) AS INTEGER

file$ = "TEST.DAT" + CHR$(0)
inarray(1) = &H3C00        'DOS system service in AX
inarray(3) = 0             'File attribute in CX
inarray(4) = SADD(file$)   'ASCIIZ string in DX

CALL INT86OLD (&H21, inarray(), outarray())
```

Related statements: CALL INT86XOLD; CALL INTERRUPT; CALL INTERRUPTX

CALL INT86XOLD Statement

Calls a DOS system service.

Syntax:

CALL INT86XOLD (*interrupt_number*, *in_array*(), *out_array*())

Notes:

Though functionally similar to INT86OLD, INT86XOLD supports 10-element arrays that store registers AX, BX, CX, DX, BP, SI, DI, FLAGS, DS, and ES.

Many DOS services require values for the DS and ES registers. The CALL INT86XOLD statement allows you to supply these values.

To use CALL INT86XOLD, you must use the QB.LIB library or the QB.QLB Quick library.

Example:

See CALL INT86OLD.

Related statements: CALL INT86OLD; CALL INTERRUPT; CALL INTERRUPTX

CALL INTERRUPT Statement

Calls a DOS system service using a user-defined record structure.

Syntax:

CALL INTERRUPT (*interrupt_number*, *inregs*, *outregs*)

Notes:

interrupt_number is a number (0 through 255) that corresponds to the desired DOS system service.

inregs and *outregs* are variables of the user-defined type RegType.

The QB.BI file defines the type RegType, which contains members corresponding to the 8086 registers:

```
TYPE RegType
     ax    AS INTEGER
     bx    AS INTEGER
     cx    AS INTEGER
     dx    AS INTEGER
     bp    AS INTEGER
     si    AS INTEGER
     di    AS INTEGER
     flags AS INTEGER
END TYPE
```

To call a DOS service, assign the corresponding register values to the members of *inregs*. When the service completes, CALL INTERRUPT assigns the ending register values to the members of *outregs*.

To use CALL INTERRUPT, you must use the QB.LIB library or the QB.QLB Quick library.

Example:

```
' Create a file named TEST.DAT  using interrupt 21H function 3CH
' $INCLUDE: 'QB.BI'
DIM inregs AS RegType, outregs AS RegType

file$ = "TEST.DAT" + CHR$(0)
inregs.ax = &H3C00        'DOS system service
inregs.cx = 0             'File attribute
inregs.dx = SADD(file$)   'Filename offset

CALL INTERRUPT(&H21, inregs, outregs)
```

Related statements: CALL INT86OLD; CALL INT86XOLD; CALL INTERRUPTX

CALL INTERRUPTX Statement

Calls a DOS system service using a user-defined record structure.

Syntax:

CALL INTERRUPTX (*interrupt_number*, *inregs*, *outregs*)

Notes:

Though functionally similar to CALL INTERRUPT, CALL INTERRUPTX allows you to specify values for the DS and ES registers.

See the type RegTypeX in the QB.BI include file.

To use CALL INTERRUPTX, you must use the QB.LIB library or the QB.QLB Quick library.

Example:

See CALL INTERRUPT.

Related statements: CALL INT86OLD; CALL INT86XOLD; CALL INTERRUPT

CDBL Function

Converts a numeric expression to a double-precision value.

Syntax:

CDBL(*numeric_expression*)

Notes:

numeric_expression is any numeric expression.

Using CDBL is equivalent to assigning the expression to a double-precision variable.

Single-precision values have 7 significant digits. Double-precision values have 15 significant digits.

Example:

```
PRINT 5 / 6
PRINT CDBL(5 / 6)
```

Running this program produces the following display:

```
.8333333
.8333333333333334
```

Related functions: CINT; CLNG; CSNG; FIX; INT

CHAIN Statement

Transfers control from one QuickBASIC program to another.

Syntax:

CHAIN *filename*

Notes:

filename is a character string containing the filename of the program to which control is to be passed.

If your program is executing within the QuickBASIC environment, the file must be a BASIC source file. If your program is executing outside the QuickBASIC environment, the file must be an executable file.

To exchange information between chained programs, you must use the COMMON statement.

After you transfer control to another program using CHAIN, the program that called CHAIN does not resume control when the chained program completes.

Example:

```
CHAIN "TEST.BAS"            'Inside QuickBASIC environment
```

Related statements: CALL; COMMON; RUN

CHDIR Statement

Changes the default directory for the specified drive.

Syntax:

CHDIR *directory_name*

Notes:

directory_name is a string expression containing the desired directory name. It must have fewer than 64 characters.

To change the default directory for a drive other than the current drive, precede the pathname with a disk drive letter and a colon.

CHDIR does not change the default drive.

You cannot abbreviate CHDIR.

Example:

```
'Change the current directory in
'drive C to \DOS
```

(continued)

```
CHDIR "C:\DOS"
```
Related statements: MKDIR; RMDIR

CHR$ Function

Returns a one-character string containing the character that corresponds to the specified ASCII value.

Syntax:

CHR$(*ascii_value*)

Notes:

ascii_value is the ASCII code of the desired character.

CHR$ is commonly used to sound the computer bell (CHR$(7)) and to terminate an ASCIIZ string so that it can be used in a DOS system service call (CHR$(0)).

The standard ASCII values range from 0 through 127. The IBM PC and compatibles support extended ASCII characters from 128 through 255. Many extended characters are useful for drawing boxes and other simple graphics.

Example:

```
'Display the ASCII and extended ASCII character sets

FOR i = 0 TO 255
    PRINT i; CHR$(i)
NEXT i
```

Related functions: ASC

CINT Function

Rounds a numeric expression to an integer value.

Syntax:

CINT(*numeric_expression*)

Notes:

numeric_expression must result in a value in the range –32,768 through 32,767. If the expression is outside this range, a run-time error occurs.

CINT rounds; it does not truncate.

Example:

```
PRINT CINT(34.51)
PRINT CINT(34.49)
```

Running this program produces the following display:

```
35
34
```

Related functions: CDBL; CLNG; CSNG; FIX; INT

CIRCLE Statement

Draws a circle or ellipse with the specified radius and center.

Syntax:

CIRCLE [STEP] (*x, y*), *radius* [, [*color*][, [*start_angle*]
[, [*end_angle*][, *aspect_ratio*]]]]

Notes:

STEP is an optional keyword that, when present, tells CIRCLE that the *x* and *y* values are offsets from the current graphics cursor position.

x, y are the coordinates of the circle's center.

radius is the radius of the circle in the current coordinate system.

color is the border color for the circle. The circle is not filled.

start_angle is the starting angle in radians for the arc. The default is 0.

end_angle is the ending angle in radians for the arc. The default is 2π.

aspect_ratio is the ratio of the length of the *y* axis to the length of the *x* axis. By changing the aspect ratio, you can create ellipses.

Example:

```
'Fill the screen with random circles
SCREEN 1
FOR i = 1 TO 100
    x = INT(320 * RND)
    y = INT(200 * RND)
```

(continued)

```
      RADIUS = INT(100 * RND)
      CIRCLE (x, y), RADIUS
NEXT i
SCREEN 0
```

Related functions: POINT

Related statements: COLOR; DRAW; LINE; PRESET; PSET; SCREEN

CLEAR Statement

Initializes all program variables, closes all files, and optionally defines the stack size.

Syntax:

CLEAR [, , *stack_size*]

Notes:

CLEAR closes all open files, sets all numeric variables and arrays to 0, and sets all string variables to zero length.

If your program uses recursion or performs several levels of subroutine calls, you might need to increase your program's stack size.

stack_size is the size of the stack in bytes. You must precede the stack size with two commas as shown.

Do not execute CLEAR within a subroutine.

Example:

```
'Initialize variables and create a stack of 4096 bytes
CLEAR , , 4096
```

CLNG Function

Rounds a numeric expression to a long (4-byte) integer.

Syntax:

CLNG(*numeric_expression*)

Notes:

numeric_expression must evaluate to a value in the range −2,147,483,648 through 2,147,483,647. If the result is outside this range, a run-time error occurs.

Example:

```
PRINT CLNG(338457.8)
PRINT CLNG(2147358.28)
```

Running this program produces the following display:

```
338458
2147358
```

Related functions: CDBL; CINT; CSNG; FIX; INT

CLOSE Statement

Closes one or more files opened by the OPEN statement.

Syntax:

CLOSE [[#]*file_number* [, [#]*file_number*]]...

Notes:

file_number is a file number associated with a specific file by means of the OPEN statement.

You can specify more than one file number in a single CLOSE statement.

Once you close a file number, you cannot use the file number for read or write operations until you open a new file.

The CLEAR, END, RESET, RUN, and SYSTEM statements close your files automatically. For housekeeping purposes, however, you should issue a corresponding CLOSE statement for each OPEN statement in your program.

Example:

```
OPEN "TEST.DAT" FOR OUTPUT AS #1
PRINT #1, "This is a test"
CLOSE #1
```

Related statements: OPEN; RESET

CLS Statement

Clears the screen display.

Syntax:

CLS [{0¦1¦2}]

Notes:

Depending on the region of the screen you want to clear, CLS gives
you four options:

Statement	Result
CLS	Clears text or graphics viewport
CLS 0	Clears entire screen of text and graphics
CLS 1	Clears only the graphics viewport
CLS 2	Clears only the text viewport, leaving the bottom line unchanged

Example:

CLS

Related statements: VIEW; VIEW PRINT; WINDOW

COLOR Statement

Sets the screen color.

Syntax:

COLOR [*foreground*][, [*background*][, *border*]]	(Screen mode 0)
COLOR [*foreground*][, *palette*]	(Screen mode 1)
COLOR [*foreground*][, *background*]	(Screen modes 7–10)
COLOR [*foreground*]	(Screen modes 12–13)

Notes:

The COLOR statement allows you to set text foreground and background colors as well as color palettes in graphics mode.

See the SCREEN statement for specifics on each screen mode.

In screen mode 0, you can set the text foreground color to one of 16
colors (0 through 15). To use the blinking version of the color, add the

value 16 to the color, yielding a value in the range 16 through 31. The background screen border must be a color value from 0 through 15.

In screen mode 1, you can specify a palette value in the range 0 through 255. The palette determines which of two sets of colors to use for graphics display.

In screen modes 7 through 10, the foreground color is an attribute number and the background color is a color number.

In screen modes 12 through 13, the foreground color is an attribute number. You cannot specify a background color.

Example:

```
SCREEN 0
FOR fcolor = 0 TO 31
    COLOR fcolor
    PRINT "Current color is"; fcolor
    INPUT dummy$
NEXT fcolor
```

Related functions: SCREEN

Related statements: PAINT; PALETTE

COM Statement

Enables or disables data communications event trapping on the specified port.

Syntax:

COM(*n*) ON

or

COM(*n*) OFF

or

COM(*n*) STOP

Notes:

n is the number of the communications port (1 or 2).

COM ON enables communications event trapping. If a character arrives at the port, your program will execute the subroutine defined by the ON COM statement.

COM OFF disables communications event trapping. Characters arriving at the port are ignored.

COM STOP prevents event trapping until the program executes a COM ON statement. Events are processed once trapping is enabled.

Example:

```
'Enable event trapping on port 1
COM(1) ON
```

Related statements: ON *event* GOSUB

COMMAND$ Function

Returns a character string containing the command line used to start the program.

Syntax:

COMMAND$

Notes:

COMMAND$ returns the command line that follows your program name. COMMAND$ removes leading blanks and converts all lower-case letters to uppercase.

The QuickBASIC Run menu allows you to specify a command line for use while you are in the QuickBASIC environment.

Example:

```
PRINT COMMAND$
```

COMMON Statement

Defines variables to be global within a module or between chained programs.

Syntax:

COMMON [SHARED] [/*common_block_name*/] *variable_list*

Notes:

The SHARED keyword states that the specified variables are shared by all subprograms and functions in a module.

common_block_name allows you to group related variables into named common blocks. To access a variable, a routine must know the common block name. You cannot use named common blocks for chaining.

variable_list is the list of global variables with variable names separated by commas. QuickBASIC allows you to specify variables as

variable_name[()] [**AS** *type*]

COMMON statements must appear before any executable statements in your program. QuickBASIC associates variables in common blocks by position, not by name.

QuickBASIC allows you to place the following *nonexecutable* statements before a common statement:

COMMON	DEF*type*	REM
CONST	DIM (for static	SHARED
DATA	arrays)	STATIC
DECLARE	OPTION BASE	TYPE…END TYPE

Example:

```
COMMON a, b, c
a = 1: b = 2: c = 3
CHAIN "COMMON.BAS"

'CODE FOR COMMON.BAS
COMMON x, y, z
PRINT x, y, z
```

Running this program produces the following display:

```
1      2      3
```

CONST Statement

Defines a symbolic constant.

Syntax:

CONST *symbol_name* = *expression* [, *symbol_name* = *expression*]…

Notes:

Constants allow your programs to use symbolic names in place of numeric or string values.

symbol_name is the name that the constant will have throughout your program. You cannot change the value of a constant once you have defined it.

expression is a numeric or string expression assigned to the constant. You cannot use variables or functions in the expression.

Constants defined in a subprogram or function are local to that subprogram or function.

Example:

```
CONST true = 1
CONST daysperweek = 7

'Use constant in array declaration
DIM Days(daysperweek)
```

COS Function

Returns the cosine of the specified angle.

Syntax:

COS(*angle*)

Notes:

angle is the angle for which you want to find the cosine.

You can express an angle in either degrees or radians. The QuickBASIC trigonometric routines support only radians. To convert degrees to radians, use the following equation:

radians = 3.141593 $*$ (*degrees* / 180)

Example:

```
angle = .785
PRINT "Cosine of"; angle; "is"; COS(angle)
```

Running this program produces the following display:

```
Cosine of .785 is .7073882
```

Related functions: ATN; SIN; TAN

CSNG Function

Converts a numeric expression to a single-precision value.

Syntax:

CSNG(*numeric_expression*)

Notes:

numeric_expression is any numeric expression.

Using CSNG is equivalent to assigning the expression to a single-precision variable.

Single-precision values have seven significant digits.

Example:

```
a# = 6
b# = 7
PRINT a#/b#, CSNG(a#/b#)
```

Running this program produces the following display:

```
 .8571428571428571          .8571429
```

Related functions: CDBL; CINT; CLNG; FIX; INT

CSRLIN Function

Returns the current cursor row number.

Syntax:

CSRLIN

Notes:

CSRLIN returns the cursor's line (row) number. POS returns the cursor's column number.

Example:

```
'Save cursor row and column
saveline = CSRLIN
savecol = POS(0)
'Move to line 10, column 20
LOCATE 10,20: PRINT "Message at 10,20"
'Restore cursor to previous position
LOCATE saveline, savecol
```

Related functions: POS

Related statements: LOCATE

CVD Function

Converts an 8-byte string (created by MKD$) to a double-precision value.

Syntax:

CVD(*eight_byte_string*)

Example:

```
OPEN "PAYROLL.DAT" FOR RANDOM AS #3 LEN = 35
FIELD #3, 27 AS names$, 8 AS salary$
GET #3, 1
PRINT "EMPLOYEE: "; name$
PRINT "Salary $"; CVD(salary$)
CLOSE #3
```

Related functions: CVDMBF; CVI; CVL; CVS; CVSMBF; MKD$

CVDMBF Function

Converts an 8-byte string containing a double-precision value (created by MKDMBF$) from Microsoft binary format to IEEE format.

Syntax:

CVDMBF(*eight_byte_string*)

Example:

See CVD.

Related functions: CVD; CVI; CVL; CVS; CVSMBF; MKDMBF$

CVI Function

Converts a 2-byte string (created by MKI$) to an integer value.

Syntax:

CVI(*two_byte_string*)

Example:

See CVD.

Related functions: CVD; CVDMBF; CVL; CVS; CVSMBF; MKI$

CVL Function

Converts a 4-byte string (created by MKL$) to a long integer value.

Syntax:

CVL(*four_byte_string*)

Example:

See CVD.

Related functions: CVD; CVDMBF; CVS; CVSMBF; MKL$

CVS Function

Converts a 4-byte string (created by MKS$) to a single-precision value.

Syntax:

CVS(*four_byte_string*)

Example:

See CVD.

Related functions: CVD; CVDMBF; CVL; CVSMBF; MKSMBF$

CVSMBF Function

Converts a 4-byte string containing a single-precision value (created by MKSMBF$) from Microsoft binary format to IEEE format.

Syntax:

CVSMBF(*four_byte_string*)

Example:

See CVD.

Related functions: CVD; CVDMBF; CVI; CVL; CVS; MKSMBF$

DATA Statement

Stores numeric and string constants to be read with the READ statement.

Syntax:

DATA *constant* [, *constant*]...

Notes:

constant is a numeric or string constant.

READ statements access DATA statements in the order the DATA statements appear in your program. The RESTORE statement allows your program to reread DATA statements as necessary.

The type of a variable in a READ statement must match the type of the constant in the DATA statement.

Example:

```
DATA 1, 2.2345, "TEST"
READ a%, b#, c$
PRINT a%, b#, c$
```

Running this program produces the following display:

```
1    2.2345    TEST
```

Related statements: READ; RESTORE

DATE$ Function

Returns a character string containing the current date in the form *mm-dd-yyyy*.

Syntax:

DATE$

Notes:

The DATE$ function returns the current date. The DATE$ statement sets the system date.

Example:

```
PRINT DATE$
```

Running this program line produces the following display:

```
01-13-1989
```

Related statements: DATE$

DATE$ Statement

Sets the system date.

Syntax:

DATE$ = *date_string*

Notes:

date_string is a string containing the desired date in the form "*mm-dd-yyyy*" where *mm* is the month (1 through 12), *dd* is the day (1 through 31), and *yyyy* is the year (1980 through 2099).

If you specify only the last two digits of the year, DATE$ assumes that the first two digits are "19."

DATE$ allows you to use either dashes or slashes to separate the date fields.

Example:

```
DATE$ = "12/25/89"
```

Related functions: DATE$

DECLARE Statement

Declares a procedure and directs the compiler to perform type checking for each parameter.

Syntax:

DECLARE {**FUNCTION** ⋮ **SUB**} *routine_name* [**CDECL**]
  [**ALIAS** "*alias_name*"] [([*argument_list*])]

Notes:

The DECLARE statement directs the compiler to ensure that the types
of parameters passed to a procedure match the types that the procedure
expects.

DECLARE is needed only when you don't use CALL or when you call
a function defined in another module.

The keyword FUNCTION indicates that the routine is a function;
likewise, SUB indicates a subprogram.

routine_name is the name of the function or subprogram.

The CDECL keyword indicates that the routine uses the C calling
convention.

The ALIAS keyword indicates that the routine has a different name —
alias_name — within the object file.

argument_list is an optional list of parameters separated by commas.
For compiler type checking, specify arguments as follows:

variable_name [**AS** *type*]

You can specify BYVAL in the argument list to pass the parameter by
value or SEG to pass the parameter using a far pointer.

Valid types include INTEGER, LONG, SINGLE, DOUBLE, STRING,
ANY, or a user-defined type. ANY allows any type for that parameter.

Example:

See CALL, CALLS Statements.

Related statements: CALL; CALL, CALLS

DEF FN Statement

Defines a function.

Syntax:

DEF FN*name* [(*argument_list*)] = *expression*

or

DEF FNname [(argument_list)]
   ⋮
FNname = expression
   ⋮
END DEF

Notes:

Function names must begin with FN and can contain up to 40 characters. The function name indicates the value type the function returns:

Function Name	*Returns*
FNday$	string
FNcount%	integer
FNaverage#	single-precision value

For a function to return a value, the function must assign its result to the function name.

argument_list is a list of parameters to the function separated by commas as follows:

argument_name [**AS** *type*]

You cannot use a function before your program defines it, nor can you use DEF FN functions recursively.

Example:

```
DEF FNsum (a AS INTEGER, b AS INTEGER) = a + b

DEF FNmax (a AS INTEGER, b AS INTEGER, c AS INTEGER)
    IF (a > b) THEN
          max = a
    ELSE
          max = b
    END IF
    IF (max > c) THEN
          FNmax = max
    ELSE
          FNmax = c
    END IF
END DEF

PRINT FNsum(3, 5)
PRINT FNmax(1, 2, 3)
```

Running this program produces the following output:

```
8
3
```

Related statements: EXIT; FUNCTION; STATIC

DEF SEG Statement

Sets the current segment address for subsequent PEEK functions and BLOAD, BSAVE, CALL ABSOLUTE, and POKE statements.

Syntax:

DEF SEG [= *address*]

Notes:

address is an integer expression in the range 0 through 65,535. If you omit *address*, QuickBASIC uses the BASIC data segment.

Example:

See CALL ABSOLUTE Statement.

Related functions: PEEK

Related statements: BLOAD; BSAVE; CALL ABSOLUTE; POKE

DEFDBL Statement

Defines the default data type as double-precision for variables whose names begin with a letter in the specified range.

Syntax:

DEFDBL *letter*[-*last_letter*][, *letter*[-*last_letter*]] ...

Notes:

letter and *last_letter* are a range of letters to associate with a type. QuickBASIC does not distinguish between uppercase and lowercase variables.

If a variable name includes %, &, !, #, or $, QuickBASIC ignores the default data type.

Example:

```
DEFDBL a-j
```

Related statements: DEFINT; DEFLNG; DEFSNG; DEFSTR

DEFINT Statement

Defines the default data type as integer for variables whose names begin with a letter in the specified range.

Syntax:

DEFINT *letter*[-*last_letter*][, *letter*[-*last_letter*]] ...

Notes:

See DEFDBL.

Example:

```
DEFINT x-z
```

Related statements: DEFDBL; DEFLNG; DEFSNG; DEFSTR

DEFLNG Statement

Defines the default data type as long for variables whose names begin with a letter in the specified range.

Syntax:

DEFLNG *letter*[-*lastletter*][, *letter*[-*last_letter*]] ...

Notes:

See DEFDBL.

Example:

```
DEFLNG l-n
```

Related statements: DEFDBL; DEFINT; DEFSNG; DEFSTR

DEFSNG Statement

Defines the default data type as single-precision for variables whose names begin with a letter in the specified range.

Syntax:

DEFSNG *letter*[-*last_letter*][, *letter*[-*last_letter*]]...

Notes:

See DEFSNG.

Example:

```
DEFSNG t-w
```

Related statements: DEFDBL; DEFINT; DEFLNG; DEFSTR

DEFSTR Statement

Defines the default data type as string for variables whose names
begin with a letter in the specified range.

Syntax:

DEFSTR *letter*[-*last_letter*][, *letter*[-*last_letter*]]...

Notes:

See DEFDBL.

Example:

```
DEFSTR s
'sdate defaults to string
sdate = DATE$
PRINT sdate
```

Related statements: DEFDBL; DEFINT; DEFLNG; DEFSNG

DIM Statement

Declares an array variable and allocates storage.

Syntax:

DIM [**SHARED**] *variable_name*[(*subscripts*)][**AS** *type*]
  [,*variable_name*[(*subscripts*)][**AS** *type*]]...

Notes:

The SHARED keyword allows subprograms and functions to share the same variable without passing the variable as a parameter.

variable_name is the name of the array.

subscripts is the dimensions of the array. By default, QuickBASIC uses the subscripts 0 to 10. You can change the lower and upper bounds as shown here:

```
DIM a(0 TO 8)        'a(0) to a(8)
DIM b(1 TO 10)       'b(1) to b(10)
```

If you specify only one subscript, QuickBASIC assumes that it is the upper bound and uses 0 for the lower bound unless you include an OPTION BASE statement.

For multidimensional arrays, simply separate the subscripts of each array dimension with commas:

```
DIM box(3, 3)
DIM bigbox(1 TO 10, 1 TO 10)
```

The maximum number of array dimensions is 60.

Valid types include INTEGER, LONG, SINGLE, DOUBLE, STRING, and user-defined types.

Example:

```
DIM a(25 TO 100) AS INTEGER
DIM b(1 TO 10, 1 TO 5) AS DOUBLE

TYPE Schedule
     day AS STRING * 10
     hours AS INTEGER
END TYPE
DIM workday AS Schedule
```

Related statements: OPTION BASE

DO UNTIL Statement

Repeats a set of instructions until a condition becomes true.

Syntax:

DO UNTIL *Boolean_expression*
    statements
LOOP

or

DO
   statements
LOOP UNTIL *Boolean_expression*

Notes:

Boolean_expression is an expression that evaluates to true or false, such as I > 100.

The first form of the statement first tests the Boolean expression. If the expression is true, QuickBASIC skips the statements within the loop and continues execution at the first statement following the loop. If the expression is false, QuickBASIC executes the statements within the loop until the expression is true.

The second form of the statement first performs the statements within the loop and then tests the Boolean expression. If the expression is false, QuickBASIC repeats the statements in the loop. If the expression is true, QuickBASIC continues execution at the first statement following the loop.

Example:

```
i = 0
DO
     PRINT i
     i = i + 1
LOOP UNTIL i = 100
```

Related statements: DO WHILE

DO WHILE Statement

Repeats a set of instructions as long as a specific condition is met.

Syntax:

DO WHILE *Boolean_expression*
   statements
LOOP

or

DO
   statements
LOOP WHILE *Boolean_expression*

Notes:

Boolean_expression is an expression that evaluates to true or false, such as N$ = "QUIT".

The first form of the statement first tests the Boolean expression. If the expression is true, QuickBASIC executes the statements within the loop until the expression becomes false. Once the expression is false, the program continues execution at the first statement that follows the loop.

The second form of the statement first executes the statements within the loop and then tests the Boolean expression. If the expression is true, QuickBASIC repeats the statements; otherwise, execution continues at the first statement after the loop.

Example:

```
i = 0
DO WHILE i < 100
     PRINT i
     i = i + 1
LOOP
```

Related statements: DO UNTIL

DRAW Statement

Draws an object specified in a string expression.

Syntax:

DRAW *string_expression*

Notes:

DRAW uses a string containing graphics commands to draw an object. The string can contain cursor, color, and scaling commands.

Cursor movement commands are as follows:

Command	Description	Command	Description
U [n]	Up n units	F [n]	Down and right n units
D [n]	Down n units	G [n]	Down and left n units
L [n]	Left n units	H [n]	Up and left n units
R [n]	Right n units	M x,y	Move to x,y
E [n]	Up and right n units		

DRAW allows you to precede the cursor movement functions with
B and N:

Command	Description
B	Move but do not draw points
N	Move but return to original position once drawn

Angle, color, and scaling commands are as follows:

Command	Description
A *rotation*	Set rotation angle in degrees: $0 = 0°, 1 = 90°, 2 = 180°, 3 = 270°$
TA *degree*	Turn an angle ($-360°$ through $360°$)
C *color*	Set color
S *n*	Set scale factor for units
P *color*, *border*	Paint the interior of the object *color* and the border of the object *border*

Example:

```
'Draw a box and fill it
SCREEN 1
DRAW "C3"
DRAW "L20U20R20D20"      'draw box
DRAW "BH10"              'move into box
DRAW "P2,3"             'paint box
```

END Statement

Ends a QuickBASIC program.

Syntax:

END

Notes:

The END statement is used with DEF, FUNCTION, IF, SELECT, SUB,
and TYPE. Those forms of END are discussed in relation to the appro-
priate statements.

END by itself terminates your program and closes all files.

Example:

```
FOR i = 1 TO 10
    PRINT i
NEXT i
END
```

ENVIRON Statement

Changes an existing entry or places a new entry in the DOS environment.

Syntax:

ENVIRON *string_expression*

Notes:

The ENVIRON statement expects a string expression of the same form as the DOS SET command: *entry=value*.

The change to the environment table is valid only for the life of the program.

Example:

```
ENVIRON "PROGRAM=TEST"
PRINT ENVIRON$("PROGRAM")
```

Running this program produces the following display:

```
TEST
```

Related functions: ENVIRON$

ENVIRON$ Function

Returns an entry from the DOS environment.

Syntax:

ENVIRON$(*entry_string*)

or

ENVIRON$(*n*)

Notes:

The DOS SET command allows you to set and display environment strings from the DOS prompt.

The first form of ENVIRON$ allows your program to access the value of an environment variable. *entry_string* is the name of the desired environment variable.

The second form of ENVIRON$ allows your program to access the *n*th environment string.

If the specified entry does not exist, ENVIRON$ returns a null string.

Example:

```
PRINT ENVIRON$("PATH")

i = 1
DO WHILE ENVIRON$(i) <> ""
    PRINT ENVIRON$(i)
    i = i + 1
LOOP
```

Related statements: ENVIRON

EOF Function

Tests for the end-of-file condition.

Syntax:

EOF(*file_number*)

Notes:

EOF returns true if the end of the file associated with the file number specified has been reached; otherwise, EOF returns false.

file_number is the number assigned to the file in its OPEN statement.

Example:

```
OPEN "\CONFIG.SYS" FOR INPUT AS #1
DO UNTIL EOF(1)
    LINE INPUT #1, fdata$
    PRINT fdata$
LOOP
CLOSE #1
```

Related statements: CLOSE; OPEN

ERASE Statement

Reinitializes the elements of a static array or deallocates dynamic arrays.

Syntax:

ERASE *array* [, *array*]...

Notes:

array is the name of the array to reinitialize or deallocate.

For static numeric arrays, ERASE sets each element to zero. For static string arrays, ERASE sets each element to null.

For dynamic arrays, ERASE frees the memory used by the specified arrays.

Example:

```
DIM a(100)
FOR i = 1 TO 100
     a(i) = i
NEXT i
ERASE a                      'Reinitialize A
FOR i = 1 TO 100
     PRINT a(i)
NEXT i
```

Related statements: DIM; REDIM

ERDEV Function

Returns an integer error code from the last device that declared an error.

Syntax:

ERDEV

Notes:

The DOS critical error handler sets the value for ERDEV. The lower byte contains the DOS error code (0 through 12). The upper byte contains bits from the device-attribute word.

Example:

```
ON ERROR GOTO Handler
  :
Handler:
    PRINT "Error accessing device "; ERDEV$
    PRINT "Error status code "; ERDEV
    :
```

Related functions: ERDEV$; ERL; ERR

Related statements: ON ERROR

ERDEV$ Function

Returns a character string containing the name of the device that generated a critical error.

Syntax:

ERDEV$

Notes:

The DOS critical error handler sets the value for ERDEV$.

Example:

See ERDEV.

Related functions: ERDEV; ERL; ERR

Related statements: ON ERROR

ERL Function

Returns the line number preceding the line causing an error.

Syntax:

ERL

Notes:

ERL returns only line numbers. It does not return line labels. If you are not using line numbers, ERL returns 0.

Example:

```
1000 Handler:
1010     PRINT "Error processing at line"; ERL
1020     PRINT "Error number"; ERR
1030     RESUME
```

Related functions: ERDEV; ERR

Related statements: ERROR; ON ERROR; RESUME

ERR Function

Returns the error code for the last error that occurred.

Syntax:

ERR

Notes:

Error Codes	Description	Error Codes	Description
2	Syntax error	50	Field overflow
3	RETURN without GOSUB	51	Internal error
4	Out of DATA	52	Bad file name or number
5	Illegal function call	53	File not found
6	Overflow	54	Bad file mode
7	Out of memory	55	File already open
9	Subscript out of range	56	FIELD statement active
11	Division by zero	57	Device I/O error
13	Type mismatch	58	File already exists
14	Out of string space	59	Bad record length
16	String formula too complex	61	Disk full
19	No RESUME	62	Input past end of file
20	Device timeout	63	Bad record number
24	Device fault	64	Bad file name
27	Out of paper	67	Too many files
39	CASE ELSE expected	68	Device unavailable
40	Variable required	69	Communication-buffer overflow

Error Codes	Description	Error Codes	Description
70	Permission denied	74	Rename across disks
71	Disk not ready	75	Path/File access error
72	Disk-media error	76	Path not found
73	Advanced feature unavailable		

Example:

See ERL.

Related functions: ERDEV; ERR

Related statements: ERROR; ON ERROR; RESUME

ERROR Statement

Simulates an occurrence of the error number specified. Allows a program to define its own error codes.

Syntax:

ERROR *numeric_expression*

Notes:

numeric_expression is an integer value in the range 0 through 255.

See the ERR statement for the list of predefined error status codes. To define your own error, use an undefined error value.

The ERROR statement assigns the error value specified to ERR and passes control to the error handler.

Example:

```
ON ERROR GOTO HANDLER
'Test error handler with error 222
ERROR 222
EndTest:
END

Handler:
        PRINT "In error handler with error"; ERR
        RESUME EndTest
```

Related functions: ERDEV; ERL; ERR

Related statements: ON ERROR; RESUME

EXIT Statements

Exit a DO or FOR loop, function, or subprogram.

Syntax:

EXIT DEF   Exit DEF FN function

or

EXIT DO   Exit a DO loop

or

EXIT FOR   Exit a FOR loop

or

EXIT FUNCTION Exit a FUNCTION procedure

or

EXIT SUB   Exit a subprogram

Notes:

For DO and FOR loops, execution continues at the first statement following the loop.

For functions and subprograms, execution continues at the statement following the statement that called the function or subroutine.

Example:

```
j = 30
FOR i = 1 TO 50
     IF i = j THEN
          EXIT FOR
     END IF
NEXT i
PRINT "Ending value is"; i
```

Running this program produces the following display:

```
Ending value is 30
```

EXP Function

Returns the exponent of an expression.

Syntax:

EXP(*numeric_expression*)

Notes:

EXP returns the base of natural logarithms (*e*) raised to the power specified by *numeric_expression*.

numeric_expression must be less than or equal to 88.02969; otherwise, EXP results in an overflow error.

Example:

```
PRINT "New salary: "; EXP(payrate)
```

Related functions: LOG

FIELD Statement

Defines a random-access file buffer.

Syntax:

FIELD [#]*file_number*, *width* **AS** *str_variable*...

Notes:

file_number is the number assigned to the file in its OPEN statement.

width is the number of characters in the field.

str_variable is the name of a string variable to be used when reading from or writing to the file.

A variable name that appears in a FIELD statement should not appear in an INPUT statement or on the left side of an assignment operator. If it does, the variable will no longer reference the random-access file buffer.

Using record variables is usually more convenient than using the FIELD statement.

Example:

```
OPEN "RANDOM.DAT" FOR RANDOM AS #1 LEN=80
FIELD #1, 76 AS name$, 4 AS salary$
```

Related statements: GET; LSET; OPEN; PUT; RSET

FILEATTR Function

Returns either the file mode or the DOS file handle for an open file.

Syntax:

FILEATTR(*file_number*, *file_info*)

Notes:

file_number is the file number assigned to a file in its OPEN statement.

file_info dictates the information FILEATTR returns. If 1, FILEATTR returns the access mode:

Value	Mode
1	Input
2	Output
4	Random
8	Append
32	Binary

If *file_info* is 2, FILEATTR returns the DOS file handle.

Example:

```
OPEN "APPEND.DAT" FOR APPEND AS #1
OPEN "OUTPUT.DAT" FOR OUTPUT AS #2

PRINT "File 1 Mode"; FILEATTR(1, 1)
PRINT "File 1 Handle"; FILEATTR(1, 2)
PRINT "File 2 Mode"; FILEATTR(2, 1)
PRINT "File 2 Handle"; FILEATTR(2, 2)
CLOSE #1: CLOSE #2
```

Running this program produces the following display:

```
File 1 Mode 8
File 1 Handle 5
File 2 Mode 2
File 2 Handle 6
```

FILES Statement

Displays the names of files in the current or specified directory.

Syntax:

FILES [*string_expression*]

Notes:

string_expression is a string expression that contains a DOS file specification of the files to display. Wildcard characters can be used.

If you omit a file specification, FILES displays the files in the current directory.

Example:

```
FILES               'List all files
FILES "*.BAS"       'List all .BAS files
FILES "A:"          'List all files on drive A
```

FIX Function

Returns the integer portion of a floating-point expression.

Syntax:

FIX(*numeric_expression*)

Notes:

numeric_expression is any numeric expression.

Example:

```
PRINT FIX(-10.99)
PRINT FIX(-10.1)
```

Running this program produces the following display:

```
-10
-10
```

Related functions: CINT; INT

FOR Statement

Repeats a given set of instructions a specific number of times.

Syntax:

FOR *control_variable* = *start_value* **TO** *end_value* [**STEP** *increment*]
   ⋮
NEXT [*control_variable* [, *control_variable*]...]

Notes:

control_variable is the variable that FOR increments with each iteration of the loop. It controls whether or not QuickBASIC repeats the loop.

start_value is the initial value that QuickBASIC assigns to the control variable.

end_value is the value that the control variable must equal before the loop ends.

increment is the amount that QuickBASIC adds to the control variable with each iteration of the loop. The increment can be a positive or negative value. If you omit *increment*, the default increment is 1.

The NEXT statement directs QuickBASIC to increment the control variable and to test whether the control variable is greater than the end value. If it is not, execution continues at the first statement within the loop; otherwise, execution continues at the first statement following NEXT.

Example:

```
FOR i = 1 TO 10
     PRINT "i ="; i
NEXT i

FOR i = 1 TO 10
     FOR j = 1 TO 10
          PRINT i; "*"; j; "="; i * j
     NEXT j
NEXT i
```

Related statements: EXIT FOR

FRE Function

Returns the amount of available stack space, string space, or memory.

Syntax:

FRE(*numeric_expression*)

or

FRE(*string_expression*)

Notes:

If the argument to FRE is −1, FRE returns the size in bytes of the largest array you can create. If the argument is −2, FRE returns the available stack space. For any other numeric argument, FRE returns the amount of available string space.

If the argument to FRE is a string expression, FRE compacts the free string space into a single block and then returns the available string space.

Example:

```
PRINT "String space"; FRE("")
PRINT "Stack space"; FRE(-2)
PRINT "Array space"; FRE(-1)
```

Running this program produces the following display:

```
String space 48460
Stack space 784
Array space 184092
```

FREEFILE Function

Returns the next available BASIC file number.

Syntax:

FREEFILE

Notes:

FREEFILE eliminates the need for hard-coding of file numbers and, accordingly, the risk of using a file number already in use.

Example:

```
filenumber = FREEFILE
OPEN "TEST.DAT" FOR OUTPUT AS filenumber
CLOSE filenumber
```

FUNCTION Statement

Declares a user-defined function.

Syntax:

FUNCTION *function_name* [(*arguments*)] [**STATIC**]
    ⋮
    function_name = expression
    ⋮
END FUNCTION

Notes:

function_name is the name of the user-defined function. The name can end with a type-declaration character (%, &, !, #, or $) to indicate the type of value it returns.

arguments is an optional list of parameters, separated by commas, to be passed to the function.

To specify the type of each variable, use the following form:

variable[()] **AS** *type*

The STATIC keyword directs QuickBASIC to save the values of the function's local variables between function calls.

For a function to return a value, the function must at some point assign an expression to the function name.

Example:

```
FUNCTION Min% (a AS INTEGER, b AS INTEGER)
     IF (a < b) then
          Min% = a
     ELSE
          Min% = b
     END IF
END FUNCTION

PRINT "Min of 5 and 3 is"; Min%(5, 3)
```

Related statements: DECLARE; DEF FN; EXIT; FUNCTION; STATIC; SUB

GET Statement (File I/O)

Reads a record from a random-access disk file.

Syntax:

GET [#]*file_number*[, [*record_number*][, *variable*]]

Notes:

file_number is the number assigned to the file in its OPEN statement.

record_number is the number of the record desired, from 1 through 2,147,483,647. If you omit a record number, GET reads the next record.

variable is the name of the variable into which GET enters the data. Usually a user-defined record variable is used.

Example:

```
TYPE SalaryRecord
     ename AS STRING * 20
     salary AS SINGLE
END TYPE

DIM employee AS SalaryRecord

OPEN "SALARY.DAT" FOR RANDOM AS #1 LEN = LEN(employee)
GET #1, 1, employee
PRINT employee.ename, employee.salary
CLOSE #1
```

Related functions: CVD; CVI; CVL; CVS; MKD$; MKI$; MKL$; MKS$

Related statements: FIELD; INPUT; LINE INPUT; LSET; PUT; RSET

GET Statement (Graphics)

Stores a graphics screen image in an array.

Syntax:

GET [STEP](*xleft*, *ytop*)-[STEP](*xright*, *ybottom*), *array*[(*index*)]

Notes:

GET stores the screen image contained in the specified rectangle.

The keyword STEP indicates that the coordinates are offsets relative to the last point plotted.

array is the name of the array in which GET should store the image.

index is the array index at which storage of the graphics image begins.

To determine the number of bytes required, use the following formula:

$$4 + INT(((xright - xleft + 1) * (bits\_per\_pixel) + 7) / 8) *$$
$$planes * ((ybottom - ytop) + 1)$$

The number of bits per pixel and the number of planes depends on the current screen:

Screen Mode	Bits per Pixel	Planes
1	2	1
2	1	1
7	1	4
8	1	4
9	1	*
10	1	2
11	1	1
12	1	4
13	8	1

*2 if 64 KB of EGA memory; otherwise 4.

Example:

```
GET (10, 20)-(20, 50), animal
```

Related statements: PUT (Graphics); SCREEN

GOSUB Statement

Directs execution to continue at a BASIC subroutine.

Syntax:

GOSUB *location*

Notes:

location is either a line number or label to branch to.

Use a RETURN statement to end a subroutine.

GOSUB is the older method of accessing subroutines. Most new programs use QuickBASIC SUB and CALL statements.

Example:

```
GOSUB Test
END
```

(continued)

```
Test:
     PRINT "In subroutine Test"
     RETURN
```

Related statements: RETURN; SUB

GOTO Statement

Branches to the specified line number or label.

Syntax:

GOTO *location*

Notes:

location is the line number or label at which execution is to continue.

Early versions of BASIC did not have DO loops, ELSE clauses for IF statements, or SELECT CASE statements. They used GOTO to implement these constructs. To improve your program's readability and simplify your debugging, restrict the use of GOTO.

Example:

```
i = 0
Start:
     PRINT "i ="; i
     INPUT "Again"; reply$
     IF reply$="N" THEN
          END
     ELSE
          i = i + 1
     END IF
GOTO Start
```

Related statements: DO; IF; SELECT CASE

HEX$ Function

Returns a character string containing the hexadecimal representation of a value.

Syntax:

HEX$(*numeric_expression*)

Notes:

Hexadecimal notation is the base 16 numbering system. It uses the numbers 1 through 9 and the letters A through F. To store the hexadecimal representation of a number, you must use a string variable.

Example:

```
'Display octal, decimal, and
'hex values from 0 to 255
FOR i = 0 TO 255
    PRINT OCT$(i), i, HEX$(i)
NEXT i
```

Related functions: OCT$

IF Statement

Provides conditional execution based on the evaluation of an expression.

Syntax:

IF *expression* **THEN** *true_statement* [**ELSE** *false_statement*]

or

IF *expression* **THEN**
    [*true_statements*]
[**ELSEIF** *expression* **THEN**
    [*true_statements*]]
⋮
[**ELSE**
    [*false_statements*]]
END IF

Notes:

The first form of the statement allows you to execute a single statement if the expression is true and a different statement if the expression is false.

The second form of the statement allows you to execute a series of statements if the expression is true and a different set if the expression is false. Also, this syntax allows you to test for a series of different conditions, one after another.

Example:

```
IF (a > b) THEN max = a ELSE max = b

IF (a > max) THEN CALL BigValue(a)

IF (day$ = "MONDAY") THEN
     CALL Meetings
     CALL Dinners
ELSE
     CALL Gym
ENDIF

IF (DAY$ = "MONDAY") THEN
     CALL Meetings
ELSEIF (DAY$ = "THURSDAY") THEN
     CALL Tickets
ELSEIF (DAY$ = "FRIDAY") THEN
     CALL Theatre
END IF
```

Related statements: SELECT CASE

INKEY$ Function

Reads a character from the keyboard.

Syntax:

INKEY$

Notes:

INKEY$ returns a null string if no character is present, a 1-byte string for standard keys, and a 2-byte string for extended keys.

For extended keys, the first character is a null character (ASCII 0) and the second is the keyboard scan code.

INKEY$ does not echo the character to the screen.

Example:

```
PRINT "Press a series of keys - F10 to stop"
DO
     DO
          k$ = INKEY$
     LOOP WHILE k$ = ""
```

(continued)

```
        IF LEN(k$) = 1 THEN
                PRINT "Letter", k$
        ELSE
                PRINT "Scan code", ASC(MID$(k$, 2, 1))
        END IF
LOOP UNTIL MID$(k$, 2, 1) = CHR$(68)          'F10 scan code
```

INP Function

Returns a byte read from an I/O port.

Syntax:

INP(*portnumber*)

Notes:

portnumber is the number associated with the desired port. It must be
in the range 0 through 65,535.

Example:

```
'Turn on speaker through port 97
saveval = INP(97)
OUT 97, saveval + 3
DO
LOOP WHILE INKEY$ = ""
OUT 97, saveval
```

Related statements: OUT

INPUT Statement

Gets keyboard input.

Syntax:

INPUT [;] ["*prompt*"{;|,}] *variables*

Notes:

A semicolon immediately after INPUT directs QuickBASIC to leave the
cursor on the same line after the user presses Enter.

prompt is the optional prompt INPUT displays on the screen.

A semicolon after the prompt directs INPUT to display a question mark after the prompt.

A comma after the prompt directs INPUT to suppress the question mark.

variables is the list of variables to input. Separate multiple variables with commas.

If the user enters a type other than the expected variable type, INPUT displays the message *Redo from start*, and the user must reenter the data.

Example:

```
'Question mark
INPUT "Enter your name and age"; uname$, age
PRINT uname$, age
'No question mark
INPUT "Enter your name and age", uname$, age
PRINT uname$, age
```

Related functions: INPUT$

Related statements: INPUT #

INPUT # Statement

Reads data from a sequential file.

Syntax:

INPUT #*file_number*, *variables*

Notes:

file_number is the number assigned to the sequential file in its OPEN statement.

variables is the list of variables in which to store data from the file.

Example:

```
OPEN "SALARY.DAT" FOR INPUT AS #1
DO WHILE NOT EOF(1)
     INPUT #1, ename$, salary
     PRINT ename$, salary
LOOP
CLOSE #1
```

Related functions: INPUT$

Related statements: INPUT

INPUT$ Function

Reads the specified number of characters from a file or the keyboard.

Syntax:

INPUT$(*num_characters*[, [#] *file_number*])

Notes:

num_characters is the number of characters for INPUT$ to read. It must be less than or equal to the record length of the file, which is 128 by default.

file_number is the number assigned to the file in its OPEN statement. If you omit a file number, INPUT$ reads from the keyboard.

Example:

```
'Display a file in UPPERCASE
OPEN "\CONFIG.SYS" FOR INPUT AS #1
DO WHILE NOT EOF(1)
     char$ = INPUT$(1, 1)
     PRINT UCASE$(char$);
LOOP
CLOSE #1
```

Related statements: INPUT; INPUT #

INSTR Function

Returns the location of the first occurrence of a string within another string.

Syntax:

INSTR([*startposition*], *searchstring*, *substring*)

Notes:

INSTR returns the character position of *substring* within *searchstring*.

startposition is the character position within *searchstring* where the search should begin. If you omit *startposition*, INSTR begins at position 1.

If INSTR locates the substring, it returns an index to the starting character. Otherwise, INSTR returns 0.

Example:

```
PRINT "SUB in SUBSTRING", INSTR("SUBSTRING", "SUB")
PRINT "X in STRING", INSTR("STRING", "X")
```

Running this program produces the following display:

```
SUB in SUBSTRING    1
X in STRING         0
```

Related functions: LEFT$; LEN; MID$; RIGHT$

INT Function

Returns the next integer value smaller than or equal to the specified numeric expression.

Syntax:

INT(*numeric_expression*)

Notes:

numeric_expression is any numeric expression.

Example:

```
PRINT INT(99.8), INT(99.1), INT(-99.2)
```

Running this program line produces the following display:

```
 99          99          -100
```

Related functions: CINT; FIX

IOCTL Statement

Transmits a device control string to a device driver.

Syntax:

IOCTL [#] *filenumber*, *control_string*

Notes:

file_number is the file number assigned to the device in its OPEN statement.

control_string is a string expression that specifies the command to send to the device.

For information on device control string information, refer to your hardware documentation.

Related functions: IOCTL$

IOCTL$ Function

Returns a control string from a device driver.

Syntax:

IOCTL$([#]*file_number*)

Notes:

file_number is the file number assigned to the device in its OPEN statement.

The information IOCTL$ returns is device dependent. For more information, see your hardware reference manual.

Related statements: IOCTL

KEY Statements

Assign string values to the function keys F1 through F12. Optionally, display the values of each key.

Syntax:

KEY *function_key*, *string_expression*

or

KEY LIST

or

KEY ON

or

KEY OFF

Notes:

function_key is the number of the desired function key. 1 corresponds to F1; 10 corresponds to F10. Use 30 and 31 to represent keys F11 and F12.

string_expression is a string of up to 15 characters that you want to assign to the function key.

Once you assign a string to a key, QuickBASIC substitutes the string each time the user presses the corresponding function key.

KEY LIST displays the entire 15 character assignment for each key.

KEY ON displays the first six letters of the key assignments across the bottom of the screen.

KEY OFF erases the display of the key assignments from the screen.

Example:

```
'Assign a string to F1
KEY 1, "F1 function key"
'Display key assignments
KEY ON
INPUT "Press the F1 key"; x$
PRINT x$
```

KEY(*n*) Statements

Enable or disable software trapping of specific keys.

Syntax:

KEY(*n*) ON

or

KEY(*n*) OFF

or

KEY(*n*) STOP

Notes:

n is the number associated with a function key, a cursor-direction key, or a user-defined key:

Value of **n**	Meaning
1 through 10	Function keys F1 through F10
11	Up arrow key

(continued)

Value of n	Meaning
12	Left arrow key
13	Right arrow key
14	Down arrow key
15 through 25	User-defined keys
30 and 31	Function keys F11 and F12

KEY(*n*) ON enables keyboard event trapping for the specified key.

KEY(*n*) OFF disables keyboard event trapping for the specified key. QuickBASIC does not queue events that occur.

KEY(*n*) STOP inhibits event trapping for the specified key. Events are processed once trapping is enabled.

After you specify keyboard event trapping for a specific key, the ON *event* statement enables keyboard trapping.

To declare a user-defined key, use the following variation of the KEY statement:

KEY *n*, **CHR\$**(*keyboardflag*) + **CHR\$**(*scancode*)

n is the number to associate with the user-defined key (15 through 25).

keyboardflag is one of the following values:

Flag	Meaning
0	No keyboard flag
1 through 3	Either Shift key*
4	Ctrl key
8	Alt key
32	Num Lock key
64	Caps Lock key
128	Extended keys on 101-key keyboard

*Key trapping does not distinguish between the left and right Shift keys.

You can add the values together to test for multiple flags simultaneously.

scancode is the scan code of the desired key.

Example:

```
ON KEY(10) GOSUB Handler
KEY(10) ON
PRINT "Press F10 to stop"
FOR i = 0 TO 100000
    PRINT i
NEXT i
```

(continued)

```
Handler:
STOP
```

Related statements: ON *event* GOSUB

KILL Statement

Deletes a file from disk.

Syntax:

KILL *file_specification*

Notes:

file_specification is a string expression specifying the file to delete. The string can contain the DOS wildcard characters ? and *.

Example:

```
KILL "TEST.DAT"

KILL "*.OLD"
```

Related statements: FILES

LBOUND Function

Returns the lowest array subscript for the specified array dimension.

Syntax:

LBOUND(*array_name*[, *dimension*])

Notes:

array_name is the name of the array of interest.

dimension is the dimension of interest for a multidimensional array. The default is 1.

Example:

```
DIM a(50 TO 100) AS INTEGER
DIM box(1 TO 3, 3 TO 6) AS INTEGER

PRINT LBOUND(a)
PRINT LBOUND(box, 1), LBOUND(box, 2)
```

Running this program produces the following display:

```
50
1    3
```

Related functions: UBOUND

Related statements: DIM

LCASE$ Function

Returns a character string containing the letters of a string expression in lowercase.

Syntax:

LCASE$(*string_expression*)

Notes:

string_expression is any string expression.

Example:

```
INPUT "Enter a string"; s$
PRINT LCASE$(s$)
```

Related functions: UCASE$

LEFT$ Function

Returns the specified number of characters beginning from the left-most character of a string.

Syntax:

LEFT$(*string_expression*, *num_char*)

Notes:

string_expression is any string expression.

num_char is the number of characters to extract from the string. It must be in the range 0 through 32,767.

Example:

```
s$ = "TEST STRING"
FOR i = 1 TO LEN(s$)
     PRINT LEFT$(s$, i)
NEXT i
```

Related functions: MID$; RIGHT$

LEN Function

Returns the number of characters in a string or the number of bytes used to store a variable.

Syntax:

LEN(*string_expression*)

or

LEN(*variable*)

Notes:

string_expression is any string expression.

variable is any variable of a type other than STRING.

Example:

```
DIM i AS INTEGER, l AS LONG
a$ = "13 CHARACTERS"
PRINT a$, LEN(a$)
PRINT "Integer"; LEN(i), "Long"; LEN(l)
```

Running this program produces the following result:

```
13 CHARACTERS  13
Integer 2      Long 4
```

LET Statement

Assigns a value to a variable.

Syntax:

[**LET**] *variable* = *expression*

Notes:

LET is an optional keyword used in assignment statements to assign a value to a variable.

Example:

```
LET a = 5
'equivalent assignment without LET
a = 5
```

LINE Statement

Draws a line or box on the screen.

Syntax:

LINE [[**STEP**](*x1*, *y1*)]-[**STEP**](*x2*, *y2*)[,[*color*][, [**B**[**F**]][, *linestyle*]]]

Notes:

LINE draws either a line using the coordinate pair (*x1*, *y1*)=(*x2*, *y2*) as endpoints or a box with (*x1*, *y1*) as one corner and (*x2*, *y2*) as the opposite corner.

The keyword STEP directs LINE to use the coordinates as an offset from the last point plotted as opposed to physical coordinates.

color is the line or box color.

B directs LINE to draw a box rather than a line.

F directs LINE to fill the box with the specified color.

linestyle is a 16-bit value whose bits determine whether or not pixels are drawn. By changing this value, you change the style of lines on your screen.

Example:

```
'Fill the screen with random boxes
SCREEN 1
FOR i = 1 TO 1000
     x1 = RND * 320
     y1 = RND * 200
     x2 = RND * 320
     y2 = RND * 200
     scolor = RND * 4
     LINE (x1, y1)-(x2, y2), scolor, BF
NEXT i
```

Related statements: SCREEN

LINE INPUT Statement

Reads in a string of up to 255 characters.

Syntax:

LINE INPUT [;] ["*prompt*";] *string_variable*

or

LINE INPUT [#]*file_number*, *string_variable*

Notes:

Although the INPUT statement interprets a comma as a separator between two entries, the LINE INPUT statement does not. The LINE INPUT statement reads all characters up to the carriage return and assigns them to a string variable.

If present, the semicolon immediately following the keyword INPUT directs LINE INPUT to leave the cursor on the same line after the user presses Enter.

prompt is an optional message that directs the user to enter data.

string_variable is the string variable to which LINE INPUT assigns the information entered.

file_number is the file number associated with the file by the OPEN statement.

Example:

```
LINE INPUT "Enter last name, first name, MI: "; fullname$
PRINT fullname$
```

Related statements: INPUT

LOC Function

Returns the current offset or record number within a file.

Syntax:

LOC(*file_number*)

Notes:

file_number is the file number associated with the desired file by the OPEN statement.

For binary files, LOC returns the current byte offset in the file. For random-access files, LOC returns the current record number. For sequential files, LOC returns the current offset, divided by 128. For a COM device, LOC returns the number of bytes in the input queue.

Example:

```
IF LOC(1) > 100 THEN CALL ReadIt(salary)
```

Related statements: SEEK

LOCATE Statement

Moves the cursor to the specified position on the screen and, optionally, sets the cursor size.

Syntax:

LOCATE [*row*][, [*column*][, [*visible*][, [*scan_start*][, *scan_stop*]]]]

Notes:

row is the number of the desired row.

column is the number of the desired column.

visible, when true, causes the cursor to be displayed. When false, it causes the cursor to be hidden.

scan_start is an integer specifying the first cursor scan line.

scan_stop is an integer specifying the last cursor scan line.

By changing the cursor scan lines, you can change the cursor size.

Example:

```
CLS
FOR i = 5 TO 20
    LOCATE i, i
    PRINT "Location is"; i; i
NEXT i
```

Related functions: CSRLIN; POS

LOCK Statement

Prevents access to all or specific portions of a file by network process.

Syntax:

LOCK [#]*file_number* [,{*record*¦[*start*] **TO** *end*}]

Notes:

file_number is the file number associated with the desired file by the OPEN statement.

For random-access files, LOCK locks the specified record or range of records. For binary files, LOCK locks the specified byte or range of bytes. For sequential files, LOCK locks the entire file.

LOCK is necessary only in network environments.

If a network program tries to access a locked record or byte, QuickBASIC generates an error.

Example:

```
INPUT "Enter record number to update"; rec
LOCK #1, rec         'Restrict access
emp.name$ = "SMITH"
PUT #1, rec
UNLOCK rec           'Allow access
```

Related statements: UNLOCK

LOF Function

Returns the number of bytes in a file.

Syntax:

LOF(*file_number*)

Notes:

file_number is the file number associated with the desired file by the OPEN statement.

You cannot use LOF with devices.

Example:

```
OPEN "\CONFIG.SYS" FOR INPUT AS #1
PRINT "File size in bytes is"; LOF(1)
CLOSE #1
```

LOG Function

Returns the natural logarithm of a numeric expression.

Syntax:

LOG(*numeric_expression*)

Notes:

numeric_expression is any numeric expression greater than 0.

The natural logarithm is the logarithm to the base *e*.

Example:

```
INPUT "Enter a number"; num
IF num > 0 THEN
     PRINT "LOG of"; num; "is"; LOG(num)
ELSE
     PRINT "Value must be greater than zero"
END IF
```

Related functions: EXP

LPOS Function

Returns the current position of the printer head within a print buffer.

Syntax:

LPOS(*printer_number*)

Notes:

printer_number is the number of the printer of interest. 1 is LPT1, 2 is LPT2, and so on.

Not all printers support LPOS.

Example:

```
FOR i = 1 TO 100
    LPRINT i;                         'Print number on same line
    IF LPOS(1) > 50 THEN LPRINT       'Start a new line
NEXT i
```

LPRINT Statement

Prints on the printer LPT1.

Syntax:

LPRINT [*output_list*][;¦,]

Notes:

output_list is a list of numeric and string expressions to be printed. Expressions must be separated by commas or semicolons.

A semicolon following the output list leaves the print head at the next character position. A comma leaves the print head at the next tab position.

Example:

```
LPRINT "This is line 1"
LPRINT "This is on";
LPRINT " line 2"
```

Running this program produces the following display:

```
This is on line 1
This is on line 2
```

Related statements: LPRINT USING; WIDTH

LPRINT USING Statement

Prints formatted output on the printer LPT1.

Syntax:

LPRINT USING *format_string*; *output_list*[; !,]

Notes:

format_string is the output format. See PRINT USING for a list of formatting characters.

output_list is a list of numeric and string expressions to be printed. Expressions must be separated by commas or semicolons.

A semicolon following the output list leaves the print head at the next character position. A comma leaves the print head at the next tab position.

Example:

See PRINT USING.

Related statements: LPRINT; PRINT USING; WIDTH

LSET Statement

Moves data into a random-access file buffer, assigns a variable of one record type to a variable of a different record type, or left-justifies the value of a string variable.

Syntax:

LSET *string_variable* = *string_expression*

or

LSET *record_variable1* = *record_variable2*

Notes:

string_variable is either a random-access file field or a string variable.

string_expression is any string expression.

record_variable1 and *record_variable2* are user-defined record variables.

Example:

```
salary = 66000
LSET e$ = MKS$(salary)
PUT #1
```

Related statements: RSET

LTRIM$ Function

Removes the leading blank characters from a string expression.

Syntax:

LTRIM$(*string_expression*)

Notes:

string_expression is any string expression.

Example:

```
PRINT LTRIM$("    Trim test")
```

Running this program line produces the following display:

```
Trim test
```

Related functions: RTRIM$

MID$ Function

Returns a substring of a string expression that begins at the specified offset location.

Syntax:

MID$(*string_expression*, *start_offset*[, *length*])

Notes:

string_expression is any string expression.

start_offset is the position of the first character of the substring.

length is the number of characters in the substring. If you omit *length*, MID$ returns all characters from *start_offset* through the end of the string.

Example:

```
a$ = "ABCDEFGHI"
PRINT MID$(a$, 1, 5)
PRINT MID$(a$, 6)
```

Running this program produces the following display:

```
ABCDE
FGHI
```

Related functions: LEFT$; LEN; RIGHT$

Related statements: MID$

MID$ Statement

Replaces a portion of a string with another string.

Syntax:

MID$(*string_variable*, *start_offset*[, *num_char*]) = *string_expression*

Notes:

string_variable is the string variable to be modified.

start_offset is the position of the first character to be replaced in the string variable.

num_char is the number of characters in the string to replace. If you omit this value, MID$ uses the length of the replacement string.

string_expression is any string expression.

Example:

```
a$ = "ABCDEF"
MID$(a$, 2, 2) = "bc"
PRINT a$
```

Running this program produces the following display:

```
AbcDEF
```

Related functions: MID$

MKD$ Function

Converts a double-precision value to an 8-byte string for output to a random-access file by PUT.

Syntax:

MKD$(*numeric_expression*)

Notes:

numeric_expression is a double-precision numeric expression.

Example:

```
OPEN "TEST.DAT" FOR RANDOM AS #1 LEN=8
FIELD #1, 8 AS sal$
salary = 60000
sal$ = MKD$(salary)
PUT #1
CLOSE #1
```

Related functions: CVD; CVI; CVL; CVS; MKI$; MKL$; MKS$

MKDIR Statement

Creates the specified DOS subdirectory.

Syntax:

MKDIR *directory_name*

Notes:

directory_name is a string expression that specifies the subdirectory to create.

Example:

```
ON ERROR GOTO CheckExists
MKDIR "TESTDIR"
PRINT "Directory TESTDIR created"
Done:
END
```

(continued)

```
CheckExists:
    IF ERR = 75 THEN
            PRINT "Directory TESTDIR already exists"
            RESUME Done
    END IF
    ON ERROR GOTO 0
```

Related statements: CHDIR; RMDIR

MKDMBF$ Function

Converts a double-precision value stored in IEEE format to an 8-byte
string containing the value in Microsoft binary format for output to a
random-access file by PUT.

Syntax:

MKDMBF$(*numeric_expression*)

Notes:

numeric_expression is a double-precision numeric expression.

Example:

See MKSMBF$.

Related functions: CVDMBF; CVSMBF; MKSMBF$

MKI$ Function

Converts an integer value to a 2-byte string for output to a random-
access file by PUT.

Syntax:

MKI$(*numeric_expression*)

Notes:

numeric_expression is an integer numeric expression.

Example:

See MKD$.

Related functions: CVD; CVI; CVL; CVS; MKD$; MKL$; MKS$

MKL$ Function

Converts a long integer value to a 4-byte string for output to a random-access file by PUT.

Syntax:

MKL$(*numeric_expression*)

Notes:

numeric_expression is a long integer numeric expression.

Example:

See MKD$.

Related functions: CVD; CVI; CVL; CVS; MKD$; MKI$; MKS$

MKS$ Function

Converts a single-precision value to a 4-byte string for output to a random-access file by PUT.

Syntax:

MKS$(*numeric_expression*)

Notes:

numeric_expression is a single-precision numeric expression.

Example:

See MKD$.

Related functions: CVD; CVI; CVL; CVS; MKD$; MKI$; MKL$

MKSMBF$ Function

Converts a single-precision value stored in IEEE format to a 4-byte string containing the value in Microsoft binary format for output to a random-access file by PUT.

Syntax:

MKSMBF$(*numeric_expression*)

Notes:

numeric_expression is a single-precision numeric expression.

Example:

```
TYPE EmpRec
     ename AS STRING * 20
     salary AS STRING * 4
END TYPE

DIM employee AS EmpRec
OPEN "SALARY.DAT" FOR RANDOM AS #1 LEN=LEN(employee)
employee.ename = "Jones"
employee.salary = MKSMBF$(65000)
PUT #1, 1, employee
CLOSE #1
```

Related functions: CVDMBF; CVSMBF; MKDMBF$

NAME Statement

Renames a file or directory on disk.

Syntax:

NAME *oldfile_name* **AS** *newfile_name*

Notes:

oldfile_name is a string expression containing the name of an existing DOS file.

newfile_name is a string expression containing the desired filename. A file with this name cannot already exist on disk.

Example:

```
NAME "OLDFILE.DAT" AS "NEWFILE.DAT"
```

Related statements: FILES

OCT$ Function

Returns a string containing the octal representation of an integer expression.

Syntax:

OCT$(*numeric_expression*)

Notes:

Octal is the base-8 numbering system.

numeric_expression is any numeric expression.

Example:

See HEX$.

Related functions: HEX$

ON ERROR GOTO Statement

Enables error handling and specifies the first line of the error handler.

Syntax:

ON ERROR GOTO *location*

Notes:

See ERR for a list of possible errors.

location is the line number or label of the first line in the handler. A line number of 0 disables error handling.

If error handling is disabled, an error results in an error message and program termination.

Example:

```
ON ERROR GOTO Handler
OPEN "NOFILE.DAT" FOR INPUT AS #1
PRINT "File opened"
CLOSE #1
Done:
END
```

(continued)

```
Handler:
    IF ERR = 53 THEN
        PRINT "File not found"
    END IF
    RESUME Done
```

Related functions: ERDEV; ERL; ERR

Related statements: RESUME

ON *event* GOSUB Statements

Specify the first line of an event-trapping subroutine.

Syntax:

ON COM(*n*) GOSUB *location*

or

ON KEY(*n*) GOSUB *location*

or

ON PEN GOSUB *location*

or

ON PLAY(*queuesize***) GOSUB** *location*

or

ON STRIG(*n*) GOSUB *location*

or

ON TIMER(*n*) GOSUB *location*

or

ON UEVENT GOSUB *location*

Notes:

The ON COM(*n*) GOSUB statement branches to the subroutine whenever characters are received at the specified serial port.

The ON KEY(*n*) GOSUB statement branches to the subroutine whenever the key associated with the specified number is pressed.

The ON PEN GOSUB statement branches to the subroutine whenever the light pen is activated.

The ON PLAY(*queuesize*) GOSUB statement branches to the subroutine whenever the number of notes in the music buffer goes from *queuesize* to *queuesize* − 1. *queuesize* must be in the range 1 through 32.

The ON STRIG(*n*) GOSUB statement branches to the subroutine whenever the specified joystick button is pressed. See STRIG Statement for valid values for *n*.

The ON TIMER(*n*) GOSUB statement branches to the subroutine whenever the specified number of seconds have passed. The number of seconds must be in the range 1 through 86,400.

The ON UEVENT GOSUB statement branches to the subroutine whenever a user-defined event occurs.

These statements do not enable event trapping; they only associate a subroutine with an event.

Example:

```
ON KEY(10) GOSUB DisplayHelp
KEY(10) ON

PRINT "Press F10 for help"
DO
     INPUT "Enter name"; n$
     PRINT n$
LOOP UNTIL n$ = "QUIT"
END

DisplayHelp:
     PRINT "Type QUIT at name prompt"
     RETURN
```

Related statements: COM(*n*); KEY(*n*); PEN; PLAY (Event Trapping); STRIG; TIMER

ON *expression* Statements

Branch to one of several locations based on the result of an expression.

Syntax:

ON *numeric_expression* **GOSUB** *location*[, *location*] ...

or

ON *numeric_expression* **GOTO** *location*[, *location*] ...

Notes:

numeric_expression is any numeric expression in the range 0 through 255. If necessary, QuickBASIC rounds the expression to an integer value.

location is the list of line numbers or labels to branch to. If the result of the numeric expression is 1, control branches to the first location. If the expression is 2, control branches to the second location, and so on. If the value does not have a corresponding label, execution continues at the next statement.

Example:

```
FOR i = 1 TO 3
     ON i GOSUB One, Two, Three
NEXT i
END
One:
     PRINT "In One"
     RETURN
Two:
     PRINT "In Two"
     RETURN
Three:
     PRINT "In Three"
     RETURN
```

OPEN Statement

Opens a file or device for input or output operations.

Syntax:

OPEN *filename* [**FOR** *access_mode*] [**ACCESS** *network_access*]
　　[*lock_type*] **AS** [#]*file_number* [**LEN**=*record_length*]

or

OPEN *mode*, [#]*file_number*, *filename*[, *record_length*]

or

OPEN "COM*n*: *basic_com com_specifics*" [**FOR** *access_mode*]
　　AS [#]*file_number* [**LEN**=*record_length*]

Notes:

filename is a string expression containing the name of the file or device to open.

access_mode specifies how the file is to be used: INPUT, OUTPUT, APPEND, RANDOM, or BINARY.

network_access provides more detail on how the file is to be used in shared-file network environments: READ, WRITE, or READ WRITE.

lock_type is the type of file locking used in shared-file environments: SHARED, LOCK READ, LOCK WRITE, or LOCK READ WRITE.

file_number is the integer number to associate with the file for read, write, and close operations.

record_length is the number of bytes in each record. For sequential files, the default is 512; for random-access files, the default is 128. The value cannot exceed 32,767.

mode is used for older BASIC programs. It is a single-letter string that specifies the access mode:

Option	*Mode*
A	Append
B	Binary
I	Input
O	Output
R	Random

n is the number of the communications port to open, either 1 or 2.

basic_com represents the basic data-communications parameters, separated by commas, in the following form:

[*baud*][, [*parity*][, [*databits*][, [*stopbits*]]]]

> *baud* is the baud rate of the device used: 75, 110, 150, 300, 600, 1200, 1800, 2400, 4800, 9600, or 19200.
>
> *parity* is the parity of the device used: N (none), E (even), O (odd), S (space), or M (mark).
>
> *databits* is the number of bits in each data word: 5, 6, 7, or 8.
>
> *stopbits* is the number of stop bits for each word: 1, 1.5, or 2.

com_specifics is a list of data-communications specifics, separated by commas:

Option	*Purpose*
ASC	Opens device in ASCII mode
BIN	Opens device in binary mode
CD[*milliseconds*]	Specifies carrier-detect timeout
CS[*milliseconds*]	Specifies clear-to-send timeout
DS[*milliseconds*]	Specifies data-set-ready timeout

(continued)

Option	Purpose
LF	Sends linefeed after each carriage return
OP[*milliseconds*]	Specifies the OPEN statement timeout period
RB[*bytes*]	Specifies the size of the receive buffer
RS	Suppresses detection of Request To Send (RTS)
TB[*bytes*]	Specifies the size of the transmit buffer

Example:

```
OPEN "TEST.DAT" FOR INPUT AS #1

f% = FREEFILE
OPEN "NEW.DAT" FOR RANDOM AS f% LEN = 80

OPEN "COM1:4800, E, 8, 1, BIN" AS #2
```

Related functions: FREEFILE

Related statements: CLOSE

OPTION BASE Statement

Sets the default lower array bound.

Syntax:

OPTION BASE {0|1}

Notes:

If you don't specify a default lower bound, QuickBASIC uses 0.
You can specify only one OPTION BASE statement per module.
For more flexibility use the TO clause in the DIM statement.

Example:

```
OPTION BASE 0
DIM a(1 TO 20)
DIM b(20)
PRINT LBOUND(a), LBOUND(b)
PRINT UBOUND(a), UBOUND(b)
```

Running this program produces the following display:

```
1        0
20       20
```

Related functions: LBOUND; UBOUND

Related statements: DIM

OUT Statement

Sends a byte to the specified port.

Syntax:

OUT *port_number, byte_value*

Notes:

port_number is an integer expression in the range 0 through 65,535 that identifies the port.

byte_value is an integer expression in the range 0 through 255 to send to the port.

Example:

See INP.

Related functions: INP

PAINT Statement

Fills a graphics screen image with the specified color or pattern.

Syntax:

PAINT [STEP](*x*, *y*)[, [*color*][, [*bordercolor*][, *background*]]]

Notes:

The keyword STEP indicates that *x* and *y* are offsets from the current graphics position as opposed to physical coordinates.

x, *y* is a set of coordinates within the graphics image.

color is the desired fill color. If you omit *color*, PAINT uses the current foreground color.

bordercolor is the color of the border surrounding the graphics image. If you omit *bordercolor*, PAINT uses *color*.

background is a string that specifies the termination boundary. If you omit *background*, PAINT uses CHR$(0).

Example:

```
SCREEN 1
LINE (10, 10)-(50, 50), 1, B
PAINT (11, 11), 2, 1
```

Related statements: CIRCLE; COLOR; LINE; SCREEN

PALETTE, PALETTE USING Statements

Change one or more colors in the color palette.

Syntax:

PALETTE [*change_color*, *new_color*]

or

PALETTE USING *array*[(*index*)]

Notes:

change_color is the attribute to change.

new_color is the new color to assign to the attribute.

array is an array of color numbers to assign to the attributes available in the current screen mode.

index is the index of the first element in the array to use in setting the palette.

If you omit all arguments, PALETTE restores the default color values.

Example:

```
PALETTE 0, 1
```

Related statements: COLOR; SCREEN

PCOPY Statement

Copies one video display page to another.

Syntax:

PCOPY *source_page*, *target_page*

Notes:

source_page is an integer expression that specifies the video display page to be copied.

target_page is an integer expression that specifies the video display page to be copied to.

The number of video display pages available is dependent on the video-memory size and video display mode.

Example:

```
'Copy video page 1 to page 3
PCOPY 1, 3
```

PEEK Function

Returns the byte stored at a specific memory offset.

Syntax:

PEEK(*offset*)

Notes:

offset is an integer expression (in the range 0 through 65,535) that specifies an offset within the current default segment.

The DEF SEG statement defines the default segment address.

Example:

```
'Save the screen's contents
DIM screensave(3999) AS INTEGER
DEF SEG = &HB800
FOR i = 0 TO 3999
      screensave(i) = PEEK(i)
NEXT i
DEF SEG
```

Related statements: DEF SEG; POKE

PEN Function

Returns the light pen coordinates.

Syntax:

PEN(*numeric_expression*)

Notes:

numeric_expression is an integer value (in the range 0 through 9) that specifies the information PEN returns:

Value	Returns
0	-1 if pen used since last call; 0 otherwise
1	The x pixel coordinate of the last pen use
2	The y pixel coordinate of the last pen use
3	Current usage: -1 if down; 0 if up
4	The last known x pixel value
5	The last known y pixel value
6	Character row where pen was last pressed
7	Character column where pen was last pressed
8	The last known character row
9	The last known character column

PEN does not work when a mouse driver is active.

Example:

```
row% = PEN(6)
column% = PEN(7)
```

PEN Statements

Enable or disable light pen event trapping.

Syntax:

PEN ON

or

PEN OFF

or

PEN STOP

Notes:

The PEN ON statement enables light pen event trapping.

The PEN OFF statement disables light pen event trapping. All light pen events are ignored.

The PEN STOP statement temporarily suspends light pen event trapping. All light pen events occurring during this period are processed once event trapping is enabled.

Example:

```
ON PEN GOSUB Handler
PEN ON
```

Related functions: PEN

Related statements: ON *event* GOSUB

PLAY Function

Returns the number of notes in the background music queue.

Syntax:

PLAY(*dummy_argument*)

Notes:

dummy_argument is any numeric argument. It simply distinguishes the PLAY function from the PLAY statement.

PLAY returns 0 when music is in foreground mode.

Example:

```
notes% = PLAY(0)
```

Related statements: ON *event* GOSUB; PLAY

PLAY Statement

Plays the tune specified by a string expression.

Syntax:

PLAY *string_expression*

Notes:

string_expression is a string expression that contains one or more of the following commands:

Octave Commands

>	Increases octave by 1 to a maximum of 6.
<	Decreases octave by 1 to a minimum of 0.
O *level*	Sets the current octave; *level* must be 0 through 6. Default is 4.

Duration Commands

L *notetype*	Sets the length of each note from 1 to 64. 1 is whole, 2 is half, and so on. Default is 4.
ML	Sets music legato.
MN	Sets music normal. This is the default.
MS	Sets music staccato.

Mode Commands

MF	Sets music to foreground. This is the default.
MB	Sets music to background. Up to 32 notes can play as the program executes.

Temp Commands

P *duration*	Specifies a pause from 1 to 64. 1 is whole, 2 is half, and so on.
T *notes*	Sets the tempo from 32 to 255. Default is 120.

Tone Commands

A–G	Plays the note specified.
N *note*	Plays a note from 0 to 84. 0 is a rest.

Suffix Commands

# or +	Turns a note into a sharp.
–	Turns a note into a flat.
.	Plays the note $^3/_2$ as long as specified.

The string expression "X"+VARPTR$(*string*) executes the music substring *string*.

Example:

```
'Play scale in 7 different octaves
scale$ = "CDEFGAB"
PLAY "L16"
FOR i = 0 TO 6
     PLAY "O" + STR$(i)
     PLAY "X" + VARPTR$(scale$)
NEXT i
```

Related functions: PLAY

Related statements: ON *event* GOSUB; PLAY (Event Trapping);
SOUND

PLAY Statements (Event Trapping)

Enable or disable play event trapping.

Syntax:

PLAY ON

or

PLAY OFF

or

PLAY STOP

Notes:

PLAY ON enables play event trapping.

PLAY OFF disables play event trapping. All events that occur are
ignored.

PLAY STOP temporarily suspends play event trapping. All play events
are processed once play event trapping is enabled.

Example:

```
ON PLAY GOSUB Handler
PLAY ON
```

Related functions: PLAY

Related statements: ON *event* GOSUB; PLAY

PMAP Function

Maps a physical coordinate to a logical coordinate defined by the
WINDOW statement or vice versa.

Syntax:

PMAP(*coordinate*, *mapping*)

Notes:

coordinate is a numeric expression of the coordinate to be mapped.

mapping specifies the type of conversion:

Value	Maps
0	Logical coordinate to physical x
1	Logical coordinate to physical y
2	Physical coordinate to a logical x
3	Physical coordinate to a logical y

Example:

```
SCREEN 1
WINDOW SCREEN (0, 0)-(100, 100)
'Convert logical to physical
x = PMAP(50, 0)
y = PMAP(50, 1)
```

Related statements: VIEW; WINDOW

POINT Function

Returns a pixel's color or coordinates.

Syntax:

POINT(*x, y*)

or

POINT(*mapping*)

Notes:

The POINT(*x, y*) function returns the color of the pixel at the *x, y* coordinate.

The POINT(*mapping*) function returns the coordinates of the graphics cursor based on the value of *mapping*.

Value	Returns
0	Physical x coordinate
1	Physical y coordinate
2	Logical x coordinate
3	Logical y coordinate

Example:

```
x% = POINT(0)
y% = POINT(1)
pcolor% = POINT(x%, y%)
```

Related statements: COLOR; SCREEN

POKE Statement

Places a byte in the specified memory location.

Syntax:

POKE *offset*, *byte_value*

Notes:

offset is the offset (from 0 through 65,535) within the current segment where you want to place the byte.

byte_value is the value (from 0 through 255) to poke into memory.

Example:

```
'Fill CGA screen with A's
DEF SEG = &HB800
FOR i = 0 TO 3999
     IF i MOD 2 = 0 THEN
          POKE i, 65      'letter A
     ELSE
          POKE i, 7       'display attribute
     END IF
NEXT i
DEF SEG
```

Related statements: PEEK

POS Function

Returns the cursor column position.

Syntax:

POS(*dummy_argument*)

Notes:

POS does not use the parameter *dummy_argument*.

Example:

```
FOR i = 1 TO 100
    IF (POS(0) > 50) THEN
        PRINT i
    ELSE
        PRINT i;         'same line
    END IF
NEXT i
```

PRESET Statement

Draws a pixel at the specified screen coordinates.

Syntax:

PRESET [**STEP**](*x, y*)[, *color*]

Notes:

The keyword STEP indicates that *x* and *y* are offsets from the last point drawn, as opposed to actual coordinates.

PRESET is similar to PSET, except that if you omit *color*, PRESET uses the background color.

If the coordinates are outside the current viewport, no point is drawn.

Example:

See PSET.

Related statements: PSET

PRINT Statement

Writes to the screen display or a file.

Syntax:

PRINT [#*file_number*,] [*output_list*][,¦;]

Notes:

file_number is the number of the file to which output is written.

output_list is a list of one or more expressions to output. The expressions can be string or numeric.

If a semicolon ends the PRINT line, the next PRINT statement continues on the same line in the next character position. If a comma ends the line, the next PRINT statement continues on the same line in the next print zone. Print zones are 14 characters in length.

Example:

```
PRINT "This is line"; 1
PRINT "This is line";
PRINT 2
PRINT "This is line", 3
PRINT "This is line",
PRINT 4
```

Running this program produces the following result:

```
This is line 1
This is line 2
This is line    3
This is line    4
```

Related statements: LPRINT; PRINT USING

PRINT USING Statement

Writes formatted output to the screen display or a file.

Syntax:

PRINT [#*file_number*,] **USING** *format_list*; *output_list*[,¦;]

Notes:

file_number is the file to which output is written.

format_list is a string expression containing one or more of the following format specifiers:

Specifier	Result
!	Displays only the first character in a string
\ \	Prints 2 + *n* characters of a string, where *n* is the number of spaces between the backslashes

(continued)

Specifier	Result
&	Displays a string of any length
#	Represents a digit position
.	Represents the decimal point position
+	Displays a plus sign for positive values and a minus sign for negative values
−	Appends a trailing minus sign to a negative number if symbol appears at the end of a numeric field
**	Replaces leading blanks with asterisks in a numeric field
$$	Precedes a numeric value with a dollar sign
**$	Replaces leading blanks with asterisks in a numeric field and precedes the value with a dollar sign
,	Places a comma after every third digit if symbol appears to the left of the decimal point
^^^^	Displays a value in exponential format
_n	Prints the character n as a literal character as opposed to a format character

Example:

```
a = 123.4567
PRINT USING "###.##"; a
PRINT USING "+###.####"; a

a$ = "ABCDEFG"
PRINT USING "!"; a$
PRINT USING "\   \"; a$
```

Running this program produces the following result:

```
123.45
+123.4567
A
ABCD
```

Related statements: LPRINT; PRINT

PSET Statement

Draws a pixel at the specified screen coordinates.

Syntax:

PSET [STEP](*x*, *y*) [, *color*]

Notes:

The keyword STEP indicates that *x* and *y* are offsets from the last point drawn, as opposed to coordinates.

color is the desired pixel color. If you omit *color*, PSET uses the current foreground color.

If the coordinates are outside the current viewport, no point is drawn.

Example:

```
SCREEN 1
COLOR 1, 2
CLS
FOR i = 1 TO 10000
    PSET(RND * 320, RND * 200), RND * 4
NEXT i
```

Related statements: PRESET

PUT Statement (File I/O)

Writes a random-access file buffer or record variable to a file.

Syntax:

PUT [#]*file_number*[, [*record_number*][, *variable*]]

Notes:

file_number is the file number associated with the file by the OPEN statement.

record_number is the record number (from 1 through 2,147,483,647) in a random-access file or the byte offset in a binary file.

variable is a variable containing the fields of the record.

Example:

```
TYPE Employee
    ename AS STRING * 20
    salary AS SINGLE
END TYPE

DIM emp AS Employee
```

(continued)

```
OPEN "SALARY.DAT" FOR RANDOM AS #1 LEN=LEN(emp)
emp.ename = "Parrish"
emp.salary = 50000
PUT #1, 1, emp
CLOSE #1
```

Related functions: CVD; CVDMBF; CVI; CVL; CVS; CVSMBF; MKD$;
MKDMBF$; MKI$; MKL$; MKS$; MKSMBF$

Related statements: GET; LSET; OPEN; RSET

PUT Statement (Graphics)

Displays a graphics image on the screen.

Syntax:

PUT [**STEP**](*x*, *y*),*array*[(*index*)][, *display_verb*]

Notes:

The keyword STEP indicates that *x* and *y* are offsets from the last point
drawn, as opposed to physical coordinates.

array is the name of the array containing the image to display.

index is the index where the graphics image begins in the array.

display_verb indicates how the image is displayed:

Verb	Action
PSET	Colors remain unchanged
PRESET	Colors are inverted
AND	A logical AND with an existing image in the same location
OR	A logical OR with an existing image in the same location
XOR	An exclusive OR of an existing image on the screen (useful for animation)

Example:

```
SCREEN 1
DIM box(1 TO 200)
x1 = 0
x2 = 10
y1 = 0
y2 = 10
```

(continued)

```
LINE (x1, y1)-(x2, y2), 2, BF    'Create a box
GET (x1, y1)-(x2, y2), box       'Save image

FOR i = 1 TO 10000
     PUT (x1, y1), box, XOR      'Move box around
     x1 = RND * 300              'screen randomly
     y1 = RND * 180
     PUT (x1, y1), box
NEXT i
```

Related statements: GET (Graphics)

RANDOMIZE Statement

Initializes the random-number generator.

Syntax:

RANDOMIZE [*seed*]

Notes:

seed is an integer expression that initializes the random-number
generator. If you omit *seed*, RANDOMIZE prompts the user to enter it.

Example:

```
'Print fifty random numbers
'using ten different seeds
FOR i = 1 TO 10
     PRINT "Seed"; i
     RANDOMIZE i
     FOR j = 1 TO 5
          PRINT RND
     NEXT j
NEXT i
```

Related functions: RND

READ Statement

Reads values from a data list and assigns the values to variables.

Syntax:

READ *variable_list*

Notes:

variable_list is a list of variables separated by commas. READ and
DATA statements work hand in hand to assign values to these
variables.

Example:

```
READ n$, age, salary
READ address$
DATA "Kellie", 21, 500
DATA "Las Vegas, Nevada"
PRINT n$, age, salary
PRINT address$
```

Related statements: DATA; RESTORE

REDIM Statement

Changes the size of a dynamic array.

Syntax:

REDIM [SHARED] *array*(*subscripts*) [**AS** *typename*]
        [**,** *array*(*subscripts*) [**AS** *typename*]]...

Notes:

You can change the size of a dynamic array but not the number of
dimensions.

The keyword SHARED indicates that the array can be used by all
procedures in the module.

array is the name of the array to resize.

subscripts specifies the array subscripts in the form

    [*lowerbound* **TO**] *upperbound*

Multiple-dimension arrays are supported.

typename is the array type: INTEGER, LONG, SINGLE, DOUBLE,
STRING, or a user-defined type.

REDIM erases the array's previous values.

Example:

```
'$DYNAMIC
DIM box (1 TO 100)
'statements
REDIM box (1 TO 200)
```

Related statements: DIM; ERASE

REM Statement

Allows explanatory comments or remarks on a program line.

Syntax:

REM *comment*

Notes:

comment is any text.

QuickBASIC ignores comment lines unless they contain compiler metacommands.

QuickBASIC supports the use of a single quotation mark in place of the REM statement.

Example:

```
REM This is a comment
'This is a comment
```

RESET Statement

Writes any data still in the file buffers to disk and closes all disk files.

Syntax:

RESET

Notes:

The CLOSE statement closes files individually; RESET closes all open files at once.

Example:

```
RESET
```

Related statements: CLOSE

RESTORE Statement

Allows READ to reuse a previously read DATA statement.

Syntax:

RESTORE [*location*]

Notes:

location is the line number or label of the DATA statement to read next. If you omit *location*, the next READ uses the first DATA statement in the program.

Example:

```
FOR i = 1 TO 5
     READ a%, b%, c%
     PRINT a%, b%, c%
     RESTORE
NEXT i
DATA 1, 2, 3
```

Related statements: DATA; READ

RESUME Statement

Continues program execution from an error-trapping handler.

Syntax:

RESUME [*location*]

or

RESUME NEXT

Notes:

location is the line number or label at which execution should continue. If you specify 0 or omit *location*, execution continues at the statement causing the error.

The keyword NEXT continues execution at the statement immediately following the statement causing the error.

Example:

```
ON ERROR GOTO Handler
OPEN "A:TEST.DAT" FOR INPUT AS #1
'statements
END

Handler:
     PRINT "Place disk containing TEST.DAT"
     PRINT "in drive A.  Press Enter."
     INPUT dummy$
     RESUME
```

Related statements: ERROR; ON ERROR GOTO

RETURN Statement

Returns control from a subroutine to the calling procedure.

Syntax:

RETURN [*location*]

Notes:

location is the line number or label at which execution should continue. If you omit *location*, execution continues at the line following the GOSUB statement or, for event handling, at the line at which an event occurred.

Every GOSUB statement must have a corresponding RETURN statement.

Example:

```
GOSUB One
GOSUB Two
END
```

(continued)

```
One:
    PRINT "In One"
    RETURN

Two:
    PRINT "In Two"
    RETURN
```

Related statements: GOSUB; ON *event* GOSUB

RIGHT$ Function

Returns the specified number of characters from the rightmost characters in a string.

Syntax:

RIGHT$(*string_expression*, *num_char*)

Notes:

string_expression is any string expression.

num_char is the number of characters to return. If *num_char* exceeds the length of the string, RIGHT$ returns the entire string.

Example:

```
A$ = "ABCDEFGHIJ"
FOR I = 1 TO 10
    PRINT RIGHT$(A$, I)
NEXT I
```

Related functions: LEFT$; MID$

RMDIR Statement

Removes the specified subdirectory.

Syntax:

RMDIR *directory_name*

Notes:

directory_name is a string expression containing the name of the directory to delete.

RMDIR works like the DOS RMDIR command. It cannot delete the current directory or a directory containing files.

Example:

```
RMDIR "A:\TEST"
```

Related statements: CHDIR; MKDIR

RND Function

Returns a single-precision random number between 0 and 1.

Syntax:

RND[(*numeric_expression*)]

Notes:

numeric_expression specifies how RND generates the next random number:

Value	Generates
Less than 0	The same number for any given *numeric_expression*
Equal to 0	The last number generated
Greater than 0	The next random number

If you omit *numeric_expression*, RND generates the next number in the sequence.

Example:

```
'Print ten random numbers
FOR i = 1 TO 10
    PRINT INT(RND * 10)
NEXT i
```

Related statements: RANDOMIZE

RSET Statement

Assigns a variable of one record type to a variable of a different record type, or right-justifies the value of a string variable.

Syntax:

RSET *string_variable* = *string_expression*

Notes:

string_variable is either a random-access file variable or a string variable.

For random-access file variables, RSET assigns a record variable of one type to another.

For string variables, RSET right-justifies the string.

Example:

```
DIM n AS STRING * 10
PRINT "ABCDE"
RSET n = "ABCDE"
PRINT n
```

Running this program produces the following result:

```
ABCDE
     ABCDE
```

Related statements: LSET

RTRIM$ Function

Removes trailing blanks from a string.

Syntax:

RTRIM$(*string_expression*)

Notes:

string_expression is any string expression.

Example:

```
a$ = "AAAA    "
b$ = "BBBB"
PRINT RTRIM$(a$); b$
```

Running this program produces the following result:

```
AAAABBBB
```

Related functions: LTRIM$

RUN Statement

Runs the program currently in memory or an existing program from disk.

Syntax:

RUN [*line_number*]

or

RUN [*file_name*]

Notes:

line_number is a line number in the current program at which execution should begin. If you omit *line_number*, RUN begins at the first line number.

file_name is a string expression containing the name of a file to execute. Within the QuickBASIC environment, the BAS extension is assumed. Outside the environment, the EXE extension is assumed.

RUN closes all files and erases all variables. To share variables, use the CHAIN statement.

Example:

```
RUN "FILENAME"
```

Related statements: CHAIN

SADD Function

Returns the offset of a string expression within the data segment.

Syntax:

SADD(*string_expression*)

Notes:

string_expression is any string variable or single element of a string array. It cannot be a fixed-length string.

SADD is often used to pass strings to routines written in other programming languages.

Example:

```
a$ = "ABCDEF" + CHR$(0)
addr = SADD(a$)
```

Related functions: VARPTR; VARPTR$; VARSEG

SCREEN Function

Returns the character or the color attribute for the character at the specified row and column.

Syntax:

SCREEN(*row*, *column*[, *get_color*])

Notes:

row and *column* are the coordinates of the character of interest.

get_color is a numeric expression. If *get_color* is true, SCREEN returns the color of the character. If *get_color* is false or is omitted, SCREEN returns the ASCII value of the character at the specified position.

Example:

```
DIM scr(1 TO 25, 1 TO 80) AS INTEGER
'Store current screen contents
FOR row = 1 TO 25
     FOR column = 1 TO 80
          scr(row, column) = SCREEN(row, column)
     NEXT column
NEXT row
```

SCREEN Statement

Defines the screen characteristics.

Syntax:

SCREEN [*screen_mode*][, [*coloroff*][, [*active_page*][, [*visual_page*]]]]

Notes:

screen_mode is an integer expression that specifies the mode of operation:

Value	Mode	Adapter
0	Text	CGA, EGA, VGA, MCGA
1	320 × 200 graphics	CGA, EGA, VGA, MCGA
2	640 × 200 graphics	EGA, VGA
3	720 × 348 graphics	Hercules*
4	640 × 400 graphics	Olivetti, AT&T 6300
7	320 × 200 graphics	EGA, VGA
8	640 × 200 graphics	EGA, VGA
9	640 × 350 graphics	EGA, VGA
10	640 × 350 graphics	EGA, VGA
11	640 × 480 graphics	VGA, MCGA
12	640 × 480 graphics	VGA
13	320 × 200 graphics	VGA, MCGA

*The Hercules driver MSHERC.COM must be loaded.

For specifics on video modes, see *Programmer's Guide to PC and PS/2 Video Systems* (Microsoft Press, 1987).

coloroff is a numeric expression. When true, it disables color on composite monitors. (Ignored in screen modes 2 and up.)

active_page is the video display page that text output and graphics commands write to.

visual_page is the video display page that appears on your screen.

Example:

```
SCREEN 1        '320 x 200 graphics
LINE (10, 10)-(20, 20), , B
```

Related statements: CIRCLE; DRAW; LINE; PAINT

SEEK Function

Returns the current file pointer position.

Syntax:

SEEK(*file_number*)

Notes:

file_number is the file number associated with the file by the OPEN statement.

For random-access files, SEEK returns a record number in the range 1 through 2,147,483,647. For binary and sequential files, SEEK returns the current byte offset.

Example:

```
position = SEEK(1)
```

Related statements: OPEN; SEEK

SEEK Statement

Sets the file pointer position for the next read or write operation.

Syntax:

SEEK [#] *file_number*, *position*

Notes:

file_number is the file number associated with the file by the OPEN statement.

position is the desired record number in a random-access file or the byte offset in a binary or sequential file. It must be in the range 1 to 2,147,483,647.

Example:

```
OPEN "SALARY.DAT" FOR RANDOM AS #1 LEN = 80
SEEK #1, 5              'Move pointer to record 5
```

Related statements: GET; OPEN; PUT

SELECT CASE Statement

Evaluates an expression and executes the corresponding block of statements.

Syntax:

SELECT CASE *test_expression*
CASE *match_expression*
    [*statements*]
[**CASE** *match_expression*
    [*statements*]
⋮
[**CASE ELSE**
    [*default_statements*]
END SELECT

Notes:

The SELECT CASE statement evaluates an expression and searches the list of possible cases for a match. If a match is found, QuickBASIC executes the statements for that case.

test_expression is a string or numeric expression to evaluate and compare to the possible cases.

match_expression is an expression to match *test_expression*. It can have the form

expression[, *expression*]...

If any of the expressions listed match *test_expression*, *statements* executes.

match_expression can also take the form

expression **TO** *expression*

This provides a range of possible values to match.

Lastly, *match_expression* can have the form

IS *relation_operator expression*

where *relation_operator* is <, >, <=, >=, =, or <>.

statements is the list of statements that execute for a matching case.

default_statements is the list of statements that execute when no matching expression is found. These statements are associated with the CASE ELSE clause.

Once the statements within a matching case execute, the program continues execution at the first statement following the END SELECT statement.

Example:

```
FOR i = 1 TO 5
     SELECT CASE i
     CASE 1
          PRINT "One"
     CASE 2, 3
          PRINT "Two or three"
     CASE IS = 4
          PRINT "Four"
     CASE ELSE
          PRINT "Five"
     END SELECT
NEXT i
```

Running this program produces the following result:

```
One
Two or three
Two or three
Four
Five
```

Related statements: IF

SETMEM Function

Changes the amount of memory allocated for the far heap.

Syntax:

SETMEM(*heap_change*)

Notes:

Other languages often use the far heap to allocate storage for dynamic objects. If you are calling routines that dynamically allocate far memory, you might need to change the amount of memory QuickBASIC allocates for the far heap.

heap_change is a numeric expression that specifies the number of bytes by which to increase or decrease the far heap.

By default, QuickBASIC allocates as much heap space as possible.

Example:

```
'Release 2000 bytes of heap space
newheap = SETMEM(-2000)
```

SGN Function

Returns a value indicating the sign of an expression.

Syntax:

SGN(*numeric_expression*)

Notes:

numeric_expression is any numeric expression. If the value of the expression is positive, SGN returns 1. If the value is negative, SGN returns −1. If the value is 0, SGN returns 0.

Example:

```
FOR i = -3 TO 3
    IF SGN(i) = -1 THEN
        PRINT i; "is negative"
    ELSEIF SGN(i) = 0 THEN
        PRINT i; "is zero"
    ELSE
        PRINT i; "is positive"
    END IF
NEXT i
```

SHARED Statement

Gives a subprogram or function access to module-level variables.

Syntax:

SHARED *variable*[AS *typename*][, *variable*[AS *typename*]]...

Notes:

By default, a subprogram or function has access to a variable only if you pass the variable as a parameter.

variable is the name of the module-level variable to share.

typename is the variable's type: INTEGER, LONG, SINGLE, DOUBLE, STRING, or a user-defined type.

Example:

```
DIM a AS INTEGER
a = 5
CALL Test
END


SUB Test
    SHARED a AS INTEGER
    PRINT "Value of variable A is"; a
END SUB
```

SHELL Statement

Temporarily exits the program to execute a DOS command or
batch file.

Syntax:

SHELL [*DOS_command*]

Notes:

DOS_command is a string expression that specifies the command to
execute. When the DOS command completes, your program continues.
If you omit *DOS_command*, SHELL displays the DOS prompt. When
you complete your work with DOS, use the DOS EXIT command to
resume your program.

Example:

```
SHELL "DIR"            'Display directory listing

SHELL                  'DOS prompt
```

SIN Function

Returns the sine of the specified angle.

Syntax:

SIN(*angle*)

Notes:

angle is a numeric expression that specifies an angle in radians.

You can express angles in either radians or degrees. The QuickBASIC trigonometric routines support only radians.

Example:

```
pi = 3.141593
PRINT "Sine of pi", SIN(pi)
PRINT "Sine of pi/2", SIN(pi / 2)
```

Running this program produces the following result:

```
Sine of pi     -3.258414E-07
Sine of pi/2    1
```

SLEEP Statement

Suspends program execution for the specified length of time.

Syntax:

SLEEP [*seconds*]

Notes:

seconds is the number of seconds the program will be suspended.

The program remains suspended until the user presses a key, the specified number of seconds expires, or an event currently being trapped occurs.

Example:

```
SLEEP 30
```

SOUND Statement

Generates a sound from the computer's speaker.

Syntax:

SOUND *frequency*, *duration*

Notes:

frequency is an integer expression (from 37 through 32,767) that specifies the sound's frequency in hertz.

duration is an unsigned integer expression (from 0 through 65,535) that specifies the length of the sound in clock ticks. A clock tick occurs 18.2 times per second.

Example:

```
FOR i = 37 TO 3000
    PRINT i
    SOUND i, 1
NEXT i
```

SPACE$ Function

Returns a string containing the specified number of spaces.

Syntax:

SPACE$(*num_spaces*)

Notes:

num_spaces is an integer expression (from 0 through 32,767).

Example:

```
FOR i = 0 TO 5
    PRINT SPACE$(i); i
NEXT i
```

Running this program produces the following result:

```
0
 1
  2
   3
    4
     5
```

Related functions: SPC

SPC Function

Skips the specified number of spaces in a PRINT or LPRINT statement.

Syntax:

SPC(*num_spaces*)

Notes:

num_spaces is an integer value (from 0 through 32,767) that specifies the number of spaces to skip.

Example:

```
FOR i = 0 TO 5
    PRINT SPC(i); i
NEXT i
```

Related functions: SPACE$

SQR Function

Returns the square root of an expression.

Syntax:

SQR(*numeric_expression*)

Notes:

numeric_expression is any non-negative numeric expression.

Example:

```
FOR i = 0 TO 100
    PRINT i, SQR(i)
NEXT i
```

STATIC Statement

Makes the specified variable local to a subprogram or function and directs QuickBASIC to preserve the variable's value between calls.

Syntax:

STATIC *variable*[**AS** *typename*][, *variable*[**AS** *typename*]]…

Notes:

variable is the name of the variable to make static.

typename is the variable's type: INTEGER, LONG, SINGLE, DOUBLE, STRING, or a user-defined type.

Example:

```
CALL Test
CALL Test
END

SUB Test
    STATIC a AS INTEGER
    PRINT a
    a = a + 1
END SUB
```

Running this program produces the following result:

```
0
1
```

Related statements: COMMON; SHARED

STICK Function

Returns a joystick's *x* or *y* coordinate.

Syntax:

STICK(*numeric_expression*)

Notes:

numeric_expression is an unsigned integer in the range 0 through 3 that specifies the desired value:

Value	Returns
0	*x* coordinate of joystick A
1	*y* coordinate of joystick A
2	*x* coordinate of joystick B
3	*y* coordinate of joystick B

x and *y* coordinates can range from 1 through 200.

You must call STICK(0) before you use 1, 2, or 3. STICK(0) records the current joystick coordinates.

Example:

```
x% = STICK(0)
y% = STICK(1)
```

STOP Statement

Ends the program at any point.

Syntax:

STOP

Notes:

A program should have only one starting and ending point. The use of STOP to end a program from different locations is strongly discouraged.

Example:

```
Handler:
     PRINT "Failed to open file on"
     PRINT "the third attempt"
     STOP
```

STR$ Function

Returns the string representation of the specified numeric expression.

Syntax:

STR$(*numeric_expression*)

Notes:

numeric_expression is any numeric expression.

Example:

```
x$ = STR$(3.2718)
PRINT x$
```

Related functions: VAL

STRIG Function

Returns the status of a joystick trigger.

Syntax:

STRIG(*numeric_expression*)

Notes:

numeric_expression is an unsigned integer (from 0 through 7) that specifies the type of information desired:

Value	Condition
0	Lower joystick A button pressed since last STRIG(0)
1	Lower joystick A button currently pressed
2	Lower joystick B button pressed since last STRIG(2)
3	Lower joystick B button currently pressed
4	Upper joystick A button pressed since last STRIG(4)
5	Upper joystick A button currently pressed
6	Upper joystick B button pressed since last STRIG(6)
7	Upper joystick B button currently pressed

If the specified condition is true, STRIG returns −1; otherwise, STRIG returns 0.

Example:

```
'Wait for user to press
'the lower button of joystick A
DO
LOOP UNTIL STRIG(0)
```

Related statements: STRIG; ON *event* GOSUB

STRIG Statement

Enables or disables joystick trapping.

Syntax:

STRIG(*button*) **ON**

or

STRIG(*button*) **OFF**

or

STRIG(*button*) **STOP**

Notes:

button is a numeric expression that specifies which joystick button to trap:

Value	Traps
0	Lower button on joystick A
2	Lower button on joystick B
4	Upper button on joystick A
6	Upper button on joystick B

STRIG(*button*) ON enables joystick trapping for the specified button.

STRIG(*button*) OFF disables joystick trapping for the specified button. All events are ignored.

STRIG(*button*) STOP temporarily disables event trapping for the specified button. Events are processed once trapping is enabled.

Example:

```
ON STRIG(0) GOSUB Handler
STRIG(0) ON
```

Related functions: STRIG

Related statements: ON *event* GOSUB

STRING$ Function

Returns a string containing the specified number of occurrences of the specified character.

Syntax:

STRING$(*num_char*, *ascii_character*)

or

STRING$(*num_char*, *string_expression*)

Notes:

num_char is the desired number of characters.

ascii_character is the ASCII code of the desired character.

string_expression is any string expression. If you provide a string, STRING$ uses the first character of the string.

Example:

```
a$ = STRING$(10, 65)
PRINT a$
```

SUB Statement

Defines the beginning of a BASIC subprogram.

Syntax:

SUB *subprogram_name* [(*parameter_list*)] [**STATIC**]

Notes:

subprogram_name is the name of the subprogram. The name can contain up to 40 characters.

parameter_list is a list of parameters in the following form:

variable[()][**AS** *typename*][, *variable*[()][**AS** *typename*]]...

The keyword STATIC directs QuickBASIC to retain the value of the subprogram's local variables between calls.

Example:

```
CALL Test (1, 5.5, "TEST")
END

SUB Test (a AS INTEGER, b AS SINGLE, c AS STRING)
     PRINT a, b, c
END SUB
```

Related statements: CALL; DECLARE

SWAP Statement

Exchanges the values of two variables.

Syntax:

SWAP *variable1*, *variable2*

Notes:

variable1 and *variable2* must be the same type.

Example:

```
a = 1
b = 2
SWAP a, b
PRINT a, b
```

Running this program produces the following result:

```
2          1
```

SYSTEM Statement

Ends the program and returns control to the operating system.

Syntax:

SYSTEM

Notes:

SYSTEM closes all open files and ends the program's execution.

Example:

```
SYSTEM
```

TAB Function

Moves the print position to the specified column.

Syntax:

TAB(*column*)

Notes:

column is the desired tab column. If the current position is beyond the
specified column, TAB moves to the column on the next line.

Example:

```
FOR i = 1 TO 10
    PRINT TAB(i); i
NEXT i
```

Related functions: SPC

TAN Function

Returns the tangent of the specified angle.

Syntax:

TAN(*angle*)

Notes:

angle is a numeric expression specifying the desired angle in radians.

You can express an angle in radians or degrees. The QuickBASIC
trigonometric routines support only radians.

Example:

```
pi = 3.141593
PRINT TAN(pi / 4)
```

TIME$ Function

Returns the current system time.

Syntax:

TIME$

Notes:

TIME$ returns an 8-character string (in the form *hh:mm:ss*) that contains the current system time.

Example:

`PRINT TIME$`

Running this program line produces a result similar to the following:

`12:23:51`

Related statements: TIME$

TIME$ Statement

Sets the current system time.

Syntax:

TIME$ = *string_expression*

Notes:

string_expression is a string expression containing the desired time in the format *hh:mm:ss*.

TIME$ allows you to specify only hours; hours and minutes; or hours, minutes, and seconds.

Examples:

`TIME$ = "12"`

`TIME$ = "12:30"`

Related functions: DATE$; TIME$

Related statements: DATE$

TIMER Function

Returns the number of seconds since midnight.

Syntax:

TIMER

Notes:

You can use TIMER with the RANDOMIZE statement to seed the random number generator.

Example:

```
RANDOMIZE TIMER
```

TIMER Statements

Enable or disable timer event trapping.

Syntax:

TIMER ON

or

TIMER OFF

or

TIMER STOP

Notes:

TIMER ON enables timer event trapping.

TIMER OFF disables timer event trapping. Timer events that occur are ignored.

TIMER STOP temporarily suspends timer event trapping. Events that occur are processed once trapping is enabled.

Example:

```
ON TIMER(10) GOSUB Handler
TIMER ON
DO
LOOP UNTIL INKEY$ <> ""
END

Handler:
     PRINT TIME$
     RETURN
```

Related statements: ON *event* GOSUB

TROFF Statement

Disables tracing of statements.

Syntax:

TROFF

Notes:

TROFF and TRON are debugging tools used by older BASIC systems. You will usually find that using the QuickBASIC debugging tools is more convenient.

Example:

TROFF

Related statements: TRON

TRON Statement

Enables tracing of statements.

Syntax:

TRON

Notes:

See TROFF

Example:

TRON

Related statements: TROFF

TYPE Statement

Creates a user-defined type.

Syntax:

TYPE *user_typename*
    element_name **AS** *typename*
    ⋮
END TYPE

Notes:

user_typename is the name of the user-defined type.

element_name is the name of one of the record's elements.

typename is the element's type: INTEGER, LONG, SINGLE, DOUBLE, STRING, or another user-defined type.

TYPE creates a template for future variable declarations. To create a variable of this type, you must use DIM, REDIM, COMMON, STATIC, or SHARED.

Example:

```
TYPE Employee
     ename AS STRING * 20
     salary AS SINGLE
END TYPE

DIM emp AS Employee

emp.ename = "Stephanie"
emp.salary = 30000
PRINT emp.ename, emp.salary
```

Running this program produces the following result:

```
Stephanie      30000
```

Related statements: COMMON; DIM; REDIM; SHARED; STATIC

UBOUND Function

Returns an array's upper bound for the specified array dimension.

Syntax:

UBOUND(*array*[, *dimension*])

Notes:

array is the name of the array of interest.

dimension is an integer value specifying the dimension of interest in a multidimensional array. If you omit *dimension*, QuickBASIC uses 1.

Example:

```
DIM a(1 TO 5, 1 TO 10, 1 TO 25)
PRINT UBOUND(a), UBOUND(a, 2), UBOUND(a, 3)
```

Running this program produces the following result:

```
5          10          25
```

Related functions: LBOUND

UCASE$ Function

Returns a string with all letters in the specified string expression in uppercase characters.

Syntax:

UCASE$(*string_expression*)

Notes:

string_expression is any string expression.

Example:

```
a$ = "aBcd#F"
PRINT UCASE$(a$)
```

Running this program produces the following result:

```
ABCD#F
```

Related functions: LCASE$

UEVENT Statements

Enable or disable user-defined event trapping.

Syntax:

UEVENT ON

or

UEVENT OFF

or

UEVENT STOP

Notes:

UEVENT ON enables user-defined event trapping.

UEVENT OFF disables user-defined event trapping. User-defined events that occur are ignored.

UEVENT STOP temporarily suspends user-defined event trapping. Events that occur are processed once trapping is enabled.

Related statements: ON *event* GOSUB

UNLOCK Statement

Unlocks portions of a shared file for access by other network programs.

Syntax:

UNLOCK [#]*file_number*[, {*record* ¦ *start* **TO** *end*}]

Notes:

file_number is the file number associated with the desired file by the OPEN statement.

record is an integer value that specifies a single record to release in a random-access file or a single byte to unlock in a binary file.

start and *end* are integer values that specify the range of record numbers to release in a random-access file or the range of bytes to unlock in a binary file.

Example:

```
OPEN "SHARED.DAT" FOR RANDOM AS #1
LOCK #1, 1 TO 10
'Perform file update operations
UNLOCK #1, 1 TO 10
CLOSE #1
```

Related statements: LOCK

VAL Function

Converts a string representation of a numeric value to the actual numeric value.

Syntax:

VAL(*string_expression*)

Notes:

string_expression is the string representation of a numeric value.

VAL stops at the first character it cannot recognize as part of a number. Valid characters are 0 through 9, the period (.), the minus sign (−), and the plus sign (+).

Example:

```
PRINT VAL("33.44")
PRINT VAL("88k")
```

Running this program produces the following result:

```
 33.44
 88
```

Related functions: STR$

VARPTR Function

Returns a variable's offset in memory.

Syntax:

VARPTR(*variable*)

Notes:

variable is the name of any variable in your program.

QuickBASIC does not guarantee that a variable will reside at the same location in memory throughout the program execution. Use VARPTR immediately before you need the offset value.

Example:

See CALL ABSOLUTE.

Related functions: VARSEG

Related statements: DEF SEG

VARPTR$ Function

Returns a string representation of a variable's offset for use in the
PLAY and DRAW statements.

Syntax:

VARPTR$(*string_variable*)

Notes:

string_variable is a string variable containing DRAW or PLAY
commands.

QuickBASIC does not guarantee that a variable will reside in the same
memory location throughout the program execution. Use VARPTR$
immediately before you need the address.

Example:

```
scale$ = "CDEFGAB"
PLAY "X" + VARPTR$(scale$)
```

Related statements: DRAW; PLAY

VARSEG Function

Returns a variable's segment in memory.

Syntax:

VARSEG(*variable*)

Notes:

variable is the name of any variable in your program.

Example:

See CALL ABSOLUTE.

Related functions: VARPTR

Related statements: DEF SEG

VIEW Statement

Defines the screen coordinates within which graphics can be
displayed.

Syntax:

VIEW [[**SCREEN**] (*x1*, *y1*)-(*x2*, *y2*)[, [*fill_color*][, *border_present*]]]

Notes:

VIEW allows you to restrict graphics output to specific coordinates on
the screen. Coordinates outside this range are not drawn.

The keyword SCREEN states that graphics coordinates are relative to
the screen, not to the viewport.

x1 and *y1* are the coordinates of one corner of the viewport; *x2* and *y2*
are the coordinates of the opposite corner.

fill_color specifies the color to fill the viewport with.

border_present is any numeric expression that, when present, directs
VIEW to draw a borderline around the viewport.

If you omit all arguments, VIEW sets the viewport to the entire screen.

The SCREEN and RUN statements set the viewport back to the entire
screen.

Example:

```
SCREEN 1
VIEW (0, 0)-(20, 20), 1, 2
LINE (10, 10)-(100, 100)
```

Related statements: CLS; SCREEN

VIEW PRINT Statement

Defines the text mode scrolling region.

Syntax:

VIEW PRINT [*top_row* **TO** *bottom_row*]

Notes:

top_row and *bottom_row* are integer values that specify the top and bottom rows of the text mode scrolling region.

If you omit all arguments, VIEW PRINT sets the scrolling region to the entire screen.

Example:

```
CLS
VIEW PRINT 5 TO 10
FOR i = 1 TO 100
    PRINT i, i, i, i
NEXT i
```

Related statements: CLS; LOCATE; PRINT

WAIT Statement

Suspends program execution until the specified bit pattern is read from an input port.

Syntax:

WAIT *port_number*, *AND_expression*[, *XOR_expression*]

Notes:

port_number is an integer expression (from 0 through 255) that specifies the port of interest.

AND_expression is an integer expression that WAIT combines with the port value using an AND operation.

XOR_expression is an integer expression that WAIT combines with the port value using an XOR operation.

Data from the specified port is first combined with *XOR_expression* if supplied. The result is then combined with *AND_expression*. If the result is zero, WAIT continues reading port values; otherwise, QuickBASIC executes the next statement.

Example:

```
WAIT 45, 64
```

WHILE/WEND Statement

Repeats a set of statements as long as the specified condition is true.

Syntax:

WHILE *condition*
   [*statements*]
WEND

Notes:

condition is a Boolean expression. As long as *condition* is true QuickBASIC executes the statements within the loop.

statements is any list of statements.

WHILE/WEND is an older looping construct. Most QuickBASIC users use DO LOOP instead.

Example:

```
i = 0
WHILE i < 100
    PRINT i
    i = i + 1
WEND
```

Related statements: DO UNTIL; DO WHILE

WIDTH Statement

Sets the number of columns on the screen or other device or sets the width of a file.

Syntax:

WIDTH [*columns*][, *lines*]

or

WIDTH #*file_number*, *columns*

or

WIDTH *device_name*, *columns*

or

WIDTH LPRINT *columns*

Notes:

columns is the number of columns. The value must be 40 or 80 for the screen.

lines is the number of rows of text that appear on the screen. The value can be 25, 30, 43, 50, or 60, depending on your display adapter and current screen mode.

file_number is the file number associated with the desired file by the OPEN statement.

device_name is a string expression that contains the name of the desired device.

The keyword LPRINT sets the number of columns for the printer.

Once you specify a width for a device, output statements automatically wrap output to the next line when the width is exceeded.

Example:

```
'EGA monitor
WIDTH 80, 43
FOR i = 1 TO 100
     PRINT i
NEXT i
```

Related statements: SCREEN

WINDOW Statement

Defines the logical coordinates for the current viewport.

Syntax:

WINDOW [[**SCREEN**] (*x1*, *y1*)-(*x2*, *y2*)]

Notes:

The keyword SCREEN inverts the screen's coordinate system such that *y* values increase in value from the top to the bottom of the screen.

The coordinates *x1*, *y1* and *x2*, *y2* specify the logical coordinates to assign to the viewport.

Example:

```
SCREEN 1
WINDOW (0, 0)-(50, 50)
LINE (10, 10)-(40, 40), 2, B
```

Related statements: SCREEN; VIEW

WRITE Statement

Writes data to the screen or a sequential file.

Syntax:

WRITE [[#]*file_number*,]*expression_list*

Notes:

file_number is the file number associated with the desired file by the OPEN statement. If you omit *file_number*, QuickBASIC writes the data to the screen.

expression_list is a list of one or more variables or expressions that are separated by commas.

WRITE places a comma between each expression in the file; the PRINT statement does not.

Example:

```
OPEN "TEST.DAT" FOR OUTPUT AS #1
WRITE #1, "TEST", 5, 3.21, "END"
CLOSE #1
```

Running this program produces the following result in TEST.DAT:

```
"TEST",5,3.21,"END"
```

Related statements: OPEN; PRINT

The manuscript for this book was prepared and submitted to Microsoft Press in electronic form. Text files were processed and formatted using Microsoft Word.

Cover design by Thomas A. Draper
Interior text design by Greg Hickman
Principal typography by Rodney Cook

Text composition by Microsoft Press in Times Roman with display in Times Roman Bold, using the Magna composition system and the Linotronic 300 laser imagesetter.